SIN AND STATUS

A Tale of Anglo-American Criminal Justice

SIN AND STATUS
A Tale of Anglo-American Criminal Justice

J H Pain

ATHENA PRESS
LONDON

SIN AND STATUS
A Tale of Anglo-American Criminal Justice
Copyright © J H Pain 2007

All Rights Reserved

No part of this book may be reproduced in any form
by photocopying or by any electronic or mechanical means,
including information storage or retrieval systems,
without permission in writing from both the copyright
owner and the publisher of this book.

ISBN 10-digit: 1 84401 941 1
ISBN 13-digit: 978 1 84401 941 0

First Published 2007 by
ATHENA PRESS
Queen's House, 2 Holly Road
Twickenham TW1 4EG
United Kingdom

Printed for Athena Press

Preface

This presentation makes no claim to original research. It is replete with borrowings from the work of leading authorities, particularly Professors H L A Hart and Gilbert Geis, hopefully adequately acknowledged. Lacking much academic baggage, it is an attempt to provoke public debate about a criminal justice system – which we aggressively proclaim to be the finest in the world – that has serious shortcomings, hitherto papered over by uninformed respect. Much needs to be done if this system is to continue to be relevant in a world where long-standing attitudes, beliefs and institutions have already had their day in court.

Contents

Prologue	9
What Amounts to Criminal Behaviour	12
Position One: Manifest Harm	12
Position Two: Legal Moralism	16
Position Three: Observance of Status	23
Harmless Criminality	29
Prostitution and Drug Use	42
Prostitution	42
Drugs	50
White-Collar Crime	55
Definition	55
Problems with Pursuing White-Collar Crime	56
The Harm	59
Epilogue	70

Prologue

Having common cause with the knight, a member of Chaucer's motley company gathered at the Tabard Inn, who above all else 'loved chivalrie, Trouthe and honour, freedom and curteisie', is it not time we too went on a pilgrimage to seek enlightenment as to the true nature and purpose of a system of criminal justice which acts on our behalf?

In Anglo-American jurisdictions,[1] the criminal justice system is arguably the most feared and intrusive weapon in the armoury of the state. It sanctions, even in peacetime, the infliction of suffering on its own people by a taking of life itself, the deprival of liberty and property, the grossest invasions of privacy and the lifelong stigma of criminality. To bestir this Leviathan, those subject to its authority anticipate, at the very least, that its use is the most appropriate and efficacious means available for dealing with any problem committed to its charge; that its impartiality, be the accused president or prostitute, is beyond question; and that there is clear description of what constitutes criminal behaviour. These three prerequisites (the last receiving separate treatment) are the concern of this inquiry into the Anglo-American system, which has been carried worldwide by the cross and the sword, undertaken by contrasting the treatment meted out to the two most pervasive areas of criminal behaviour, namely, victimless crime (harmless criminality) and white-collar crime.

Los Angeles is the capital of the film and television industry. In its studios women hired by the casting department of entertainment moguls indulge in actual – not simulated – sexual activities with whatever man happens to be cast as their opposite

---

[1] 'Anglo-American' is a reference to those jurisdictions which have inherited the English common law. The inclusion of South Africa may raise academic eyebrows but is justified inasmuch as the focus for present purposes is upon the adjectival rules, particularly the adoption of the adversarial model.

number. These acts of prostitution,[2] routine in 'adult' productions marketed for millions of viewers worldwide, occur in a country where, with the exception of the state of Nevada, prostitution is a crime.

Meanwhile, Heidi Fleiss is running a call girl service which, perversely, receives the full attention of the criminal law. The service is perhaps too successful, much patronised by the local Hollywood community and the favoured clients of international corporations flown in by private jet. Indeed, a number of the girls involved are able to pay their way through college on their earnings.

There are, of course, some distinguishing features between the two activities: the entertainment offered by Ms Fleiss is conducted not in the presence of others but privately; it affords a modicum of choice; and the comparatively small reward is frequently put to good use. But both share an important characteristic, namely, that no one is harmed in any way in what is otherwise a notoriously violent place, recording over 400 homicides annually. However, Ms Fleiss unwisely fails to 'cooperate' with the police in the running of the business, and the federal tax authorities decide that they are not getting their cut of the takings. Charged in the federal court with eight counts of conspiracy and tax evasion, and in the state court for pandering (a medieval word for procuring), she is sentenced to a staggering term of six years' imprisonment (three in each court). This takes some getting used to: the law in one court approving prosecution by the tax collector for not receiving enough from what a woman does, while in another punishing her for doing it.

While Heidi is serving her time in the penitentiary, the financial world is once again stricken by a series of corporate scandals which shatter the lives of many thousands of defrauded investors and undermine international business confidence. Outraged, we await the exercise of the awesome power of the criminal justice system to strike down the dangerous predators responsible, as it has done in the case of the harmless transgressions of that scarlet woman, Heidi Fleiss, and her flock.

But it is not to be. The criminal law has washed its hands of

---

[2] Defined p.42.

both surveillance and control of this entire area of criminal activity, termed 'white-collar crime', leaving the task to innumerable regulatory agencies with limited authority. Police investigation followed by raids and arrest, confrontation with a jury and their victims in open court before the majesty of the bench and confinement in a prison cell, are not considered appropriate for already privileged and politically influential malefactors. It would be naive to believe that recent dramatic developments in America[3] have altered overnight a value system enshrined in law for centuries which scoffs at notions of fair play and equal justice for all.

Is this what we expect from our criminal law? Does this tale reveal a medieval system still preoccupied with carnal sin and social status?

---

[3] The Sarbanes-Oxley legislation, considered p.68.

What Amounts to Criminal Behaviour

At the outset, there is the unpalatable and unconstitutional fact that there is no substantive definition of crime, no agreement as to what constitutes criminality, no settled view about where to draw the line between the interests of the state and those of the individual. All we have is three wildly divergent positions regarding the purposes of prosecution and punishment, here termed 'manifest harm', 'legal moralism', and 'observance of status'.

Position One: Manifest Harm

John Stuart Mill's essay, *On Liberty*, published in 1859, can be viewed as a valiant attempt to halt the loss of personal freedom occasioned by the use of the criminal law as an instrument of state aggrandisement. Alarmed by the tendency to employ punishment as an instrument of first choice to suppress all behaviour deemed undesirable, Mill declared:

> The only purpose for which power can rightfully be exercised over any member of a civilised community, against his will, is to prevent harm to others. His own good, either physical or moral, is not a sufficient warrant. He cannot rightfully be compelled to do or forbear because it will be better for him to do so, because it will make him happier, because in the opinions of others, to do so would be wise or even right.[1]

At the heart of this statement of the proper function of the criminal law is the conviction that the stigma of criminality is different from and independent of any judgment that behaviour is unconventional, immoral or sinful. There can be no justification

---

[1] Quoted by H L A Hart in *Law, Liberty and Morality*, Stanford University, Oxford University Press, 1962, p.4.

for employing such a coercive, oppressive and ineffective instrument as the criminal sanction to suppress behaviour simply because it is, by some, deemed offensive but is, in other respects, harmless. With the obvious limitation, stressed by Mill, to persons 'in the maturity of their faculties',[2] the criminal justice system should confine its attention to preventing demonstrable harm to others, either in their person or property, leaving to more appropriate agencies the task of coping with activities considered merely as deviations from some moral code.

What constitutes 'harm' is a notoriously difficult question, but the answer need not detain us as this is not the issue. What is of concern is, first, whether the harm done, if any, warrants the imposition of criminal sanctions and, secondly, who is the victim of such perceived harm. All law students have some acquaintance with the rules relating to causation, whereby the law sets strict limits on legal responsibility for an injury caused in fact because, as we have been told, 'no man is an island'. Everything that we do has a ripple effect and it is necessary to draw a line between what are termed 'immediate' or 'direct' consequences and those more remote and imponderable, to which legal liability does not attach. However, the Anglo-American criminal justice system exhibits no such restraint when dealing with practices, particularly of a sexual nature, that in the words of H L A Hart, 'involve nothing that would ordinarily be thought of as harm to other persons'.[3] Also, it should not be overlooked that Mill did not allege the absence of any discernable harm but that diligent search did not reveal sufficient injury to justify the imposition of criminal sanctions.

No doubt it may be argued that an adulterous couple, a woman who terminates her pregnancy, or the drug abuser, gambler and prostitute undergo at least some loss of self-respect, (and their immediate family may suffer some adverse comment or circumstance); but to prosecute such persons as perpetrators of their own harm is, to say the least, a novel way of dealing with the situation. Yet this is precisely what the criminal law does in the whole area of what is termed 'victimless crime'. Of course, it would greatly simplify the task of the prosecuting authorities if attention were

---

[2] Ibid. at p.5.
[3] Ibid. at p.25.

always confined to the victims of crime. The targets of, say, rape and robbery are easily identified and evidence of their involvement is obvious. Even a case of homicide need not deter us. Not so long ago we were accustomed to casting the suicide into unhallowed ground or spread-eagled at crossroads, confiscating their property and leaving their bereaved relatives destitute.

Crimes are supposed to have victims and, in the event that conjuring up the concept of victim as perpetrator is intellectually unsatisfying, the system pulls from the hat society itself. This stratagem, however, leaves unexplained the way in which an entity, which has no existence apart from its constituents, can be damaged while all its flesh and blood members remain unscathed. It also carries no health warning of the potential for brainwashing involved in the device of personification. If, indeed, the justification for persecuting otherwise harmless behaviour is the wellbeing of 'society as a whole', then, as will be explained later, we have shot ourselves in the foot.

Professor H L A Hart, formerly Professor of Jurisprudence at the University of Oxford, and other distinguished authors and committees have supported Mill's view of the proper function of the criminal law. Hart asks:

> Is the mere expression of moral condemnation a thing of value in itself to be pursued at this cost? The idea that we may punish offenders against a moral code, not to prevent harm or suffering or even the repetition of the offence but simply as a means of venting or emphatically expressing moral condemnation, is uncomfortably close to human sacrifice as an expression of religious worship.[4]

Herbert L Packer warns that 'the criminal sanction, inflicting as it does a unique combination of stigma and loss of liberty, should be resorted to only sparingly in a society that regards itself as free and open'.[5] Norval Morris and Gordon Hawkins recommend that we:

> ...strip off the moralistic excrescences of our criminal justice system so that it may concentrate on the essential. The prime function of the criminal law is to protect our persons and our

---

[4] Taken from Hart, *Law, Liberty and Morality*, pp.65–6.
[5] *The Limits of the Criminal Sanction*, Stanford University Press, 1968, pp.249–50.

property... When the criminal law invades the spheres of private morality and social welfare, it exceeds its proper limits at the cost of neglecting its primary tasks. This unwarranted extension is expensive, ineffective, and criminogenic.[6]

Even in America, where there is a marked tendency to criminalise everything deemed distasteful, the Law Institute, when it published its draft Model Penal Code (un-enacted) in 1955, recommended that all consensual relations between adults in private should be excluded from the scope of the criminal law. It referred to 'the *secular* interests of the community',[7] and 'the fundamental question of the protection to which every individual is entitled against state interference in his personal affairs when he is not hurting others'.[8]

These sentiments were reaffirmed two years later, in England, by the Wolfenden Committee:

> [T]he function [of the criminal law] ... is to preserve public order and decency, to protect the citizen from what is offensive and injurious and to provide sufficient safeguards against exploitation or corruption of others, particularly those who are specially vulnerable because they are young, weak in body or mind or inexperienced. Unless a deliberate attempt is to be made by society, acting through the agency of the law, to equate the sphere of crime with that of sin, there must remain a realm of private morality and immorality which is, in brief and crude terms, not the law's business. To say this is not to encourage private immorality.[9]

In addition to bearing a striking resemblance to Mill's appeal, this approach emphasises an important difference between activities conducted in private and their public display. In recent years, however, the distinction between private immorality and public indecency has been lost sight of. In 1995, Divine Brown, a black

---

[6] *The Honest Politicians Guide to Crime Control*, University of Chicago Press, 1970, p.2, quoted in *Victimless Crimes*, Schur and Bedau, Prentice Hall, 1974, p.10.
[7] Italics author's own.
[8] Taken from Hart, *Law, Liberty and Morality*, p.15.
[9] Taken from the report of the Committee on Homosexual Offences and Prostitution (Cmnd 247), 1957. See also p.22

woman, was imprisoned for six months and fined US$1,350 for providing Hugh Grant (the English actor) with safe oral sex in the back seat of Grant's BMW parked in the early hours of the morning in a secluded residential street in Los Angeles.[10] The conviction was for lewd behaviour, the essence of which is the public nature of the activity (not that the prosecution needs to show that the activity could have been seen), yet, if this fleeting exchange for which Ms Brown, a mother of three, was paid US$60 had occurred before a packed auditorium of theatre-goers or beneath the glare of lighting equipment before the director, camera crew and innumerable other onlookers, there would have been far greater financial reward and, perhaps, even artistic acclaim.

Attorneys Gloria Allred and Lisa Bloom point out:

> The lines that our society has drawn in the name of morality have become absurd. A woman may agree to sexual acts with men she doesn't love as long as she does not directly charge them for sex. She may legally pose nude for money, genitalia displayed for photographers. She may dance nude, as provocatively as the customer likes, for money. She may engage in sexual acts for money with men she does not know or like in erotic films, magazines or before a live audience.[11]

Clearly, Ms Brown was a victim of her social status at the bottom of the pecking order, punished for who she was and not for what she did, unless some significance is attached to the difference between a B-movie and a BMW. It will become apparent that in the attempt to exorcise the 'sins of the flesh', the criminal justice system has always viewed the status within the community of the practitioner as more relevant than the nature of the practice itself.

Position Two: Legal Moralism[12]

Mill's view of the purpose of criminal prosecution has received little recognition in the Anglo-American criminal justice system.

---

[10] Details taken from *Victimless Crime?* Robert F Meier and Gilbert Geis, Roxbury Publishing Company, 1997, pp.35–6.

[11] Meier and Geis, *Victimless Crime?* p.37.

[12] Borrowed from Hart, *Law, Liberty and Morality*, p.6.

The dominant theme, forcefully articulated by the English judiciary, is that the criminal law, in the words of Hart, 'may properly be used to punish immorality as such, even if it causes no harm to others'.[13] Harmless deviation from a society's moral code, especially sexual transgressions, warrant the imposition of criminal sanctions, whatever the cost in personal freedom and human misery.

In 1873, the Victorian judge James Fitzjames Stephen published what was intended as a crushing riposte to Mill's essay *On Liberty*. In his book *Liberty, Equality and Fraternity*, Stephen insisted that provided it was backed by an 'overwhelming moral majority' there was nothing to be said for limiting the criminal law to 'acts dangerous to society':

> Criminal law in this country actually is applied to the suppression of vice and so to the promotion of virtue to a very considerable extent: and this I say is right. There are acts of wickedness so gross and outrageous that self-protection apart they must be prevented as far as possible at any cost to the offender and punished if they occur with exemplary severity. Criminal law is in the nature of a persecution of the grosser forms of vice.[14]

Such an extreme position is not surprising when it is realised that the English law had only recently emerged from a period of unparalleled savagery, with more than 200 capital crimes, public floggings and transportation for life. The Royal Justices of Assize, clad in ermine and scarlet befitting the majesty of the law, went out from London into the shires to amaze the peasantry and hang by the neck those condemned for stealing a chicken. However, almost a century later when much had changed, Lord Devlin, in surprisingly similar vein, mounted a further judicial attack, this time aimed at the Report of the Wolfenden Committee which, incidentally, had achieved nothing other than a tightening of the controls exercised over prostitution. In his essay, *The Enforcement of Morals*, Lord Devlin declared that society has a right to punish 'immorality as such'. This is justified because 'a recognised

---

[13] *Law, Liberty and Morality*, op. cit. Preface.
[14] Taken from Hart, *The Morality of the Criminal Law*, The Hebrew University of Jerusalem, OUP, 1965, p.33, and *Law, Liberty and Morality*, pp.60 and 78.

morality is as necessary to a society's existence as a recognised government'. A person indulging in immoral behaviour, even in private, though 'no menace to others' may nevertheless 'threaten one of the great moral principles on which society is based'. Furthermore, 'history' tells us that:

> ...the loosening of moral bonds is often the first stage of disintegration. There are no theoretical limits to the power of the state to legislate against treason and sedition and likewise I think there can be no theoretical limits to legislation against immorality. Society is justified in taking the same steps to preserve its moral code as it does to preserve its government and other essential institutions ... the suppression of vice is as much the law's business as the suppression of subversive activities.[15]

It is clear that the hapless Ms Brown had no idea of the enormity of her offence; she remarked at the time, in a lingerie advertisement putting a finger on feminine concerns, that if wives and girlfriends did not make themselves more attractive their men folk might seek out women like her. However, thirty years earlier, the House of Lords left Shaw[16] in no doubt. Convicted of a conspiracy to corrupt public morals (an offence disinterred from its eighteenth-century grave) for his somewhat amateurish publication of a *Ladies' Directory* (prompted by the crackdown on the nocturnal habits of prostitutes in the aftermath of the Wolfenden Report)[17] their Lordships declared that it was a proper function of courts of law to act as general censor and guardian of public manners and strike down any behaviour which might 'lead another morally astray'.[18]

A conspiracy charge has always been one of the most feared in the criminal calendar. Its use sends a clear message to an accused person that the prosecution is in deadly earnest. It is frequently invoked to deal with traditional crime (even to the extent of inventing it where it plainly does not exist, as was done with

---

[15] Taken from Hart, *The Morality of the Criminal Law* at pp.37–8 and *Law, Liberty and Morality*, p.50.
[16] *Shaw v DPP* [1962] AC 220.
[17] The Street Offences Act 1959.
[18] *Law, Liberty and Morality*, p.10.

Shaw), whereas in so-called 'white-collar crime' the takeover by a regulatory regime (examined later) has seen its demise, although the arrangements between the usual participants (the company itself, auditors, financial consultants, legal advisors and investment bankers) reek of it. In the recent collapse of WorldCom, many of the players were in bed together – but not in any damaging and shocking sexual sense. Shaw, on the other hand, who had actually enquired of the police, who were non-committal, as to the legality of his paltry enterprise, was sent down for nine months on a trumped-up charge.

It is ironic that both Divine Brown and Heidi Fleiss[19] came to grief in Los Angeles, the centre of the film and television industry, because in recent years the artistic world has tired of portraying life and adopted the less challenging course of presenting the reality itself. This development does not augur well for the future of drama school. Of much greater significance, however, is evidence of the growth of a subculture which grossly warps important values. The prevalence of these will be discussed later when we examine white-collar crime, but it should be noted here that film buffs and critics, including Margaret Pomeranz of SBS television, required police restraint in their bid to ensure the distribution of a film containing scenes of actual sexual intercourse and acts of indecency with children, while the likes of Ms Brown, not being members of Hugh Grant's profession, languish in a prison cell.

There are serious difficulties with the view that the criminal law is some kind of moral crusade. At the outset, the Christian conscience has never been troubled by profiting from immoral or criminal activities. The earnings of prostitutes, for example, have always been a considerable source of income. In earlier times, the trade was licensed and supervised by the bishops of Westminster, and subsequently by Parliament. In Europe, the profits of licensed brothels were shared between the civic authorities and the universities. Today, regressive communities enjoy the best of both worlds. Content to ban the occupation, thereby avoiding any supervisory responsibility, they have nevertheless not relinquished the income, a slice of which is collected by the tax

---

[19] See the prologue.

authorities. Also, the sums collected via the 'revolving door' policy, whereby prostitutes are routinely arrested, fined and released to recoup their loss, are a not inconsiderable source of funds.

Again, in the modern secular state, morality and law are viewed as distinct agencies of social control. In terms of this dispensation, the criminal law is a pragmatic and coercive means of ensuring, as best it can, the essentials of social order by punishing those who are a demonstrable threat to others. The courts are not a forum for moral debate; indeed, time and time again judges have been obliged to warn counsel that they preside over a court of law, not morals. However, and without attempting to define the beast, it is unarguable that morality has biblical roots and that religious teaching has infiltrated the legal system. Indeed, as Meier and Geis point out, 'virtually every criminal statute in the Massachusetts Bay Colony appended a Biblical reference to indicate its irrefutable authority'.[20] If behaviour was not covered in the *Laws and Liberties of Massachusetts*, issued in 1648, it was declared that it should be dealt with 'according to biblical doctrine'.

Such observance has hanged adulterers, mutilated the tongues of blasphemers, desecrated the mortal remains of suicides for thwarting God's will, and punished gamblers for substituting human judgment for divine wisdom. In our lifetime, it has banned 'the Devil's brew', denied termination of pregnancies even to victims of rape, and incarcerated for life boys and girls condemned as 'moral defectives' for, respectively, personal abuse and bearing an illegitimate child.

Equally controversial are the broad assumptions made by Stephen and Lord Devlin that there exists within society an overwhelming moral majority so obvious as to make any investigation of public opinion superfluous; that such a moral majority is essential to the survival of any given society; and that the criminal law is the most appropriate method of sustaining it. Taking these allegations seriatim, it may well be that any such moral consensus is simply a projection of the moral preferences of the social class to which the holder belongs, or merely a construction of church

---

[20] *Victimless Crime?* p.10.

or state in pursuance of their agenda of control. Support for the latter is found in Meier and Geis: 'Criminal law,' they assert, 'draws its dictates from the moral preferences of those in a position to determine its content.'[21] As for the notion that such consensus is essential to survival, the causes of social disintegration have been debated for many years, but the assumption that the civilisations of the past have succumbed because of the activities of the likes of Messrs Brown, Fleiss and Shaw has never been seriously entertained. All such conjecture, however, misses the point of Mill's thesis, namely that, though many may shrink from homosexuality, from the killing of the unborn foetus and from payment for sexual services, it does not follow that the imposition of criminal sanctions, violating, as they do, our privacy and personal freedom, and inflicting misery and lasting degradation, is the appropriate course to pursue. To accept this argument requires a belief that we can be coerced into virtue, or that as Hart puts it, 'morality is best taught by fear of punishment'.[22]

Apart from the questionable value of an imposed conformity, there is the danger that if our values become entirely shored up by the criminal law they may simply wither away, leaving the law alone to set the standard. It is in this sense that the law should confine itself to enforcing what Jellinek in 1872 termed the 'minimum ethic', that is, maintaining the popular notion of 'law and order', leaving to other agencies the task of inculcating the values promoting decency and humanity in our social intercourse with others.

The claim that the criminal law is a factor in creating and maintaining values is presented without benefit of any historical verification and confers upon it a significance wholly undeserved. It is generally accepted that our values are learned at an early age, in the home and at school, and are the result of centuries of living together. They are, quite simply, essential to any cooperative existence and successful personal life.[23] They require an awareness of the desires, expectations and reactions of others and call for

---

[21] Ibid.
[22] *Law, Liberty and Morality*, p.58.
[23] Ibid. p.71.

self-discipline and restraint in a reciprocal environment. They are not static or embalmed in moral codes but constantly adapt to changing conditions, requiring refinement as we move from a rural to an urban setting and from a settled to a more mobile population. Because the legal moralist considers that the criminal law has played, and continues to play, a significant role in this evolutionary process, he proceeds to make the untenable claim that where the law does not condemn it will be seen to condone,[24] thereby ushering in a period of immorality and permissiveness leading, inevitably, to the disintegration of society.

As a justification for enlisting the blunt instrument of the criminal law, this amounts to a crass false alternative, as it ignores all those agencies of social disapproval which are so much more effective in curbing what is perceived to be undesirable behaviour. To offer but one example: the enormous success of the campaign against the smoking of cigarettes is a well-nigh perfect instance of a dramatic change in attitude wrought, in one lifetime, entirely by community displeasure informed by educational programmes, advertising campaigns and medical warnings.

The Wolfenden Committee rebutted the 'condemn or condone' fallacy,[25] but nevertheless it persists in the face of all the evidence that the intervention of the criminal law only makes matters far, far worse. The national disgrace of Prohibition gave birth to gangland America. The two most violent periods in the United States over the past hundred years coincide with the banning of alcohol and the current drug war; the homicide rate peaking at 9.7 and 10 per 100,000 respectively – a doubling of the normal rate.[26] Before 1914, drug addiction was confined to a tiny minority, and prior to the crackdown starting in 1910 with the Mann Act, reward for sexual favours was an inconsequential recreation, but these activities have been transformed by the impact of criminalisation. At vast public expense, and supported by somewhat aptly termed 'vice squads', the criminal law has succeeded in creating billion-dollar underworld enterprises. Now that they are the heartland of organised crime, we have become accustomed to armed conflicts, not only local but

---

[24] See *The Morality of the Criminal Law*, pp.39, 42–6, 84 for discussion of this notion and mention of some of its protagonists.
[25] See p.15.
[26] Source: US Census Data and FBI Uniform Crime Report.

overseas, the latter involving all the accoutrements of modern warfare, an environment breeding violence and corruption and a burgeoning of international trafficking in both product and persons.

In stark contrast, more enlightened communities have legalised prostitution and its salutary prerequisite, the brothel, and much drug use, with predictable results. For example, it is well known that the 'red-light district' (a media coinage) of Amsterdam is patronised almost exclusively by tourists attracted by fruit forbidden elsewhere, and operates free of the associated criminal activities habitually caused by the law in punitive jurisdictions.

It would be easy to account for this blatant disregard of such an escalation in crime by attributing it to the moralist's notorious indifference to facts and an impatience with questions of effectiveness induced by the need to reaffirm the faith. However, it is argued that there is a more sinister explanation.

Position Three: Observance of Status[27]

There are two competing theories about the cause of criminal law. The order theory regards the criminal justice system as a factor serving the public interest and common good, whereas the conflict theory views it as an instrument of the powerful, designed to maintain the dominance of the ruling class.

Strong support for the conflict theory comes from the pen of Professor Reiman, who claims in *The Rich get Richer and the Poor get Prison*[28] that the criminal justice system has as its purpose the creation of a large and visible criminal class drawn from the lowest socio-economic group. It is programmed to fail through the proliferation of prisons guaranteeing recidivism, the absence of any serious measures of crime reduction such as gun control, and the essentially criminogenic and futile prosecution of petty offenders, particularly in areas of high demand, like prostitution. In a similar vein, Erickson offers the insight that society benefits from deviance and promotes it while overtly desiring to stamp it out.[29]

---

[27] 'Status' is not used here in its strict legal sense but as meaning position or standing in the community.
[28] Second edition, John Wiley & Sons, 1984.
[29] KT Erickson, *Wayward Puritans*, John Wiley & Sons, 1966, p.4.

It can be argued that just as the early Church, in the business of salvation, needed a plentiful supply of sinners, so the embryonic state, in the business of power, required a steady stream of offenders, drawn from the ranks of the politically powerless, to legitimise the status quo and instil a sense of social solidarity. To these ends, it was essential that any threat was seen to come from below, diverting fear and hostility away from the upper echelons of society downwards to a common enemy.

Criminality thus became a low-life phenomenon, the product of poverty and slums. This perception persists, even though more than half a century ago, Edwin H Sutherland in his groundbreaking work on white-collar crime, exposed its untenable nature by revealing the prevalence of criminal behaviour in the upper classes; yet Aristotle, centuries earlier, had warned that 'the greatest crimes are caused by excess and not by necessity'.[30]

Building on the undoubted success of the Church in demonising the 'sins of the flesh', the state in turn targeted the selfsame activities, and harmless crimes became a large and important component of the criminal law. Having no injured party – no corpse, wound, damaged or stolen property (none of which can be ignored) – these are ideally suited: one can have as much or as little as is required. The task of getting the balance right was assisted by the emergence, in the nineteenth century, of a professional police force, replacing earlier local attempts at crime control, and supervision was left entirely in the hands of this new body. Such untrammelled discretion created a state of lawlessness at the threshold of the system and led to endemic corruption. Added to this sorry state of affairs is the incontrovertible fact that the attempt to control victimless crime has been essentially criminogenic, spawning a host of other criminal activities. It is also prohibitively expensive, outstripping in public money and police time that devoted to all other traditional crime because, due to the nature of such misdemeanours, they require constant surveillance, trapping operations ('stings'), undercover agents and the use of informants.

In striking contrast, white-collar criminality or 'organisational crime' described by Al Capone as 'the legitimate rackets', is not a police matter. As Geis and Meier remark:

---

[30] *Politics*, trans. JEC Welldon, London, Macmillan, 1932, Book II, Chapter 7, p.65.

> Nobody is tapping the telephone at General Motors and making the transcripts available to a prurient public. And neither the FBI nor the CIA is employing undercover agents to infiltrate the Chrysler Corporation or Alcoa to discover what alleged conspiracies are being hatched in violation of the criminal law.[31]

Indeed, in Australia recently, the Australian Competition and Consumer Commission, one of the agencies charged with protecting us from white-collar crime, has been called upon to apologise for a 'raid' on oil companies suspected, on the allegations of a whistle-blower, of price fixing. Apparently, such behaviour, actually filmed by the media, has caused widespread dismay and consternation within the community and mutterings about unacceptable breach of constitutional rights. No such reaction has been evident in 'drug busts' which come up empty-handed.

To ensure that the offending corporate executive is, if possible, spared the grubbiness of the criminal courts, the entire area has been cordoned off. A novel regulatory regime has been introduced, consisting of warnings, injunctions, cease-and-desist orders, orders to refund ill-gotten gains (an indulgence not shown to the common-or-garden thief) and, as a last resort, fines and loss of licence. An important component of this miscellany of sanctions, though not for the squeamish, is the 'consent decree' whereby the recalcitrant miscreant undertakes not to offend again without admitting that he offended in the first place, leaving the company free to defend any civil actions brought by aggrieved investors.

It is fashionable to claim that corporate fraud does not generate substantial public outrage, but this alleged apathy is seldom put to the test of jury trial. Why is this so? The answer lies in the regulatory regime itself and its working relationship with the prosecuting authority. The latter is dependent on what the relevant investigative agency decides to refer to it, and these agencies are loath to refer the more complicated cases because of the delay, inaction and low conviction rate attendant upon doing so. For its

---

[31] *White-Collar Crime: Offences in Business, Politics and the Professions*, the Free Press, (revised edition), 1977, p.3.

part, the prosecuting authority is reluctant to take them on as they invariably involve large numbers of sophisticated, amply funded and well-represented individuals. A blowing of the budget and blotting of its success rate is not worth the risk. In the upshot the 'minnows' (e.g. welfare cheats) are netted by the courts while the 'big fish' are admonished 'in house' by the agency. On those rare occasions when corporate executives charged with fraud have appeared before criminal courts, they are spared the usual public spectacle of the accused confronted by their flesh and blood victims (or grieving relatives). These, many but diffuse, can with little effort be found, but they are kept hidden by a deliberate focus on breach of the regulations and regulatory regime, thereby diverting attention away from the vanished lifesavings, lost homes and blighted futures.

The legal moralist may well be panicked by the ministrations of Ms Brown in the back seat of a BMW, but organisational crime violates trust and, as such, may undermine an entire socio-economic system, even democratic government. Early on, Ross referred to 'modern mutualism': the vulnerability created by increasingly complicated forms of interdependence within society, leaving us with no alternative but to entrust many of our vital interests to others.[32]

In the evolution of the conflict theory, it is impossible to overstate the role of the media in bolstering the image of criminality as a low-class activity. Skilled in the connotation of language, the white-collar criminal is nowhere described as 'deviant', 'delinquent' or 'morally defective'. Not for them those borrowings from adventure books for boys of 'rackets', 'loot' and 'jailbirds'. Exploiting our Christian heritage, television screens are filled with drug raids and murdered streetwalkers, with 'vice' providing the staple of our diet. Long-running programmes such as *Vice Girls*, *Vice Squad* and *Miami Vice*, provide that same diversion as did the bread and circuses of earlier times, while the depredations of the corporate elite pass unnoticed, tucked away in the business columns of our morning read.

Although less racially explicit than earlier fare portraying drug-crazed black youths, white slavery and Chinese opium dens, the misleading images projected by the media of the offender and the

---

[32] Edward A Ross, *Sin and Society*, Houghton Mifflin, 1907, p.14.

offence are crucial to the anathemising process. Housebreaking has sometimes been given as an example, accompanied by vandalism, excrement and physical violence, although such occurrences are exceptional. However, it is in the realm of harmless criminality, particularly prostitution, that television has staked its claim as the natural successor of the Church in recapturing the religious frenzy of the medieval mind. With special effects unavailable to the pulpit, the 'scarlet woman', now the focus of all evil in an increasingly morally conflicted world, beckons from the shadows. Here at least is the certitude that in her embrace we shall lose our immortal soul. We smell the brimstone, feel the heat and see the reflected glow of those eternal fires. Quite different is the presentation of the corporate fraudster who appears sartorially anonymous, sober and conventional.

Fear of the lower orders is factored in everywhere. It is as if we live in a beleaguered city stoutly defended by the embattled forces of law and order. New Yorkers retire at night, full of dread – as was Lord Devlin – of some seismic quake of immorality, only to awake on the morrow to find, as a consequence of some financial sleight of hand a few blocks away, that they have lost the roof over their heads.

Unchastened by the truth that in human affairs, unlike much of the natural world, the rot starts at the top, the media gives prominence to bouts of aggressive policing at street level. These campaigns, dubbed 'zero tolerance', no doubt serve as a prerequisite to any local or state election, but the jury is still out on the question of whether they have any impact on the incidence of serious crime.[33] It takes a leap of faith to believe that harassing hookers and graffiti artists and moving on beggars, drunks and loiterers has the desired effect, as these malcontents are hardly likely to graduate to the suites of presidents, be they political or corporate. Admittedly, the 1990s saw a reduction in violent crime but, unfortunately for the faithful, similar drops were recorded in cities where such high visibility policing did not take place, for example in Washington DC. More likely contenders for an improvement in quality of life awards were contemporaneous

---

[33] See the symposium on 'Why is Crime Decreasing', *Journal of Criminal Law and Criminology*, Northwestern University School of Law, vol. 88, no. 4/1988.

falls in unemployment, demographic change, changes in patterns of drug use and policies of urban renewal. The New York experiment, where arrests of petty offenders went up by 21% was accorded international coverage but no such emphasis was given to the worrying fact that the decline in crime coincided with an investigation, by the Mollen Commission, into the widespread corruption within the NYPD. 'The turnaround of the NYPD,' wrote Bratten, 'was the catalyst for the turnaround of New York City itself.'[34]

The human condition allows disadvantage; few have the same life chances, but the criminal justice system promises impartiality and even-handedness in adjudicating between the weak and the strong. Above the Law Courts in the Strand, and courts throughout the Western world, the figure of justice, blind, with scales, proclaims to all who enter, irrespective of rank, that they will receive equal treatment under the law. In similar vein, equal justice under law is carved into the edifice of every courthouse in the United States.

According to the conflict theory, however, this is not the purpose of the exercise. It is about the *punishment of status* – not what is done but who did it – deferring to the strong and vilifying the weak. It invites us to compare the fate of the powerful predator, usually a regular church-goer, a good club man on the board of the local hospital and active in charitable works, who arrives by limousine to attend a committee of inquiry into massive frauds accompanied by a team of legal heavyweights, with that of the prostitute or drug abuser, brought unwashed before a criminal court after a night in the cells. It asks us to consider whether the Anglo-American system believes that to imprison respectable and privileged professionals is unacceptable, whereas gaol is the appropriate place for the 'criminal classes' who are more accustomed to poor living conditions.

---

[34] Ibid., William J Bratten, *TURNAROUND: How America's Top Cop Reversed the Crime Epidemic*, pp.310–311.

Harmless Criminality

This category of crime, frequently termed 'victimless crime', is created, in the words of Schur, 'when we attempt to ban ... the exchange between willing partners of strongly desired goods or services.'[1] Their outstanding characteristic is that they are non-predatory: there is not only no intention to cause harm or disadvantage to another, but there is no injured party and therefore no complainant. Their existence demonstrates the seemingly irresistible urge by some to use the criminal law to dictate how we all should live, thereby constituting a repudiation of Mill's liberal thesis that, provided we cause no injury to others, we should be allowed to do as we please. In sum, they are the criminalisation of sins secularised as social problems.

Writing in 1963, Hart notes:

> Both in England and in America the criminal law still contains rules which can only be explained as attempts to enforce morality as such: to suppress practices condemned as immoral by positive morality, though they involve nothing that would ordinarily be thought of as harm to other persons. Most of the examples come from the sphere of sexual morals...[2]

That these offences are harmless, posing no threat to others, is acknowledged by both Stephen and Lord Devlin; but this is concealed by the trick of attributing to them all the evils which flow from their criminalisation. For example, prostitution is a problem only because the innocuous activity of charging for sexual favours, admittedly at bargain-basement prices,[3] has been

---

[1] Edwin M Schur and Hugo Bedau, *Victimless Crimes*, Prentice Hall, 1974, p.6.
[2] *Law, Liberty and Morality*, p.25.
[3] See Kinsey, *Sexual Behaviour in the Human Male*, 1948, p.608, where he compares the cost of guaranteed sexual release with the expense of unpredictable intercourse resulting from courtship.

proscribed. It is a sorry tale of the growth of criminal organisations which feed off these banned areas of high demand. Drug use, as well as alcohol, prostitution and gambling, have always been the most lucrative areas for organised crime, which withers away in the presence of regulated legalisation. What room is left for the criminal underworld where licensed taverns are open most of the day, medical dispensaries guarantee both quality and safe administration of drugs, legitimate casinos and lotteries ensure fair practices, and brothels, in selected areas, secure the health and safety of both provider and customer? There is also much evidence that the demand drops off faced with an available supply. Yet the regime imposed upon us refuses to yield to the self-evident truth expressed by Norval Morris: 'It is impossible to regulate behaviour that you prohibit.'[4]

It is indisputable that thriving criminal organisations, endemic police corruption and a marked increase both in violence and disease have been the legacy of an inappropriate use of the criminal law. They are the collateral damage of deliberate policy, fortified by the extraordinary claim that this imposition of criminal sanctions is but an example of the law pursuing a paternalistic course – that it is done for their own good. Dishonesty of this magnitude cannot go unchallenged because it calls into question the nature of the Christian contribution to our society.

The AIDS epidemic is largely the result of a refusal to treat drug addiction as a health issue. Even measures to curb the spread of infection through the sharing of needles, such as needle exchange programmes and the setting up of safe injecting premises, have met with fierce resistance. The staggering increase in prison population in the US is directly related to the law and order approach to drug use,[5] and it is common knowledge that gaols are breeding grounds for AIDS and other diseases such as TB. Prison construction has become a major industry. Many are

---

[4] 'Crimes Without Victims: The Law is a Busybody', *New York Times*, 28 January 1973, p.11.
[5] In 1973 drug law violation accounted for 328,670 arrests. By 2001 these accounted for 1,586,902 (with only 627,132 arrests for all violent crime). Source: *FBI Uniform Crime Report* 1973 and 2001.

now privatised but, unlike hotels, it is unnecessary to keep a watchful eye on occupancy levels as the prison population has multiplied fourfold in the past thirty years,[6] with the imposition of longer sentences for possession of ever smaller quantities of drugs. The enforcement effort is now directed at users[7] and at the local level as the major suppliers fragment and become increasingly inaccessible beyond national boundaries. In American cities the battle is waged street by street and block by block, each trashed and all occupants arrested, by contingents (some eighty in number) of armed police in riot gear. This situation would never be tolerated in the affluent white suburbs, where the hard core of chronic users live, estimated as some 5 million, and who constitute the mainstay of the trade.

In support of the intervention of the criminal law in what is a personal decision, it has always been alleged that prostitutes spread disease. This attempt to superimpose some semblance of rationality upon a crusade engendered by a pious bigotry is exposed by the circumstance that the charge has lost none of its virulence, though confronted by the arrival of antibiotics and widespread use of the condom. The incidence of venereal diseases is far more widespread among the general population indulging in casual affairs, and research undertaken during the 1990s reveals that not one prostitute working in Nevada's thirty-seven licensed brothels, where weekly medical checks are routine, tested HIV positive, compared with 57% in stateside New Jersey and 26.6% in Miami who did.[8] Nevada is the only state in America that survived the clampdown on prostitution and banning of brothels, which was complete by 1915. Elsewhere, prostitutes are dissuaded from carrying condoms because, on arrest, their possession is used as evidence that they are working in the trade.[9]

This adoption of perverse policy is typical of the twentieth century and is the result of a number of related factors, such as two great wars leading to much economic hardship and social

---

[6] *The Economist*, 10 August 2002, p.13.
[7] 80.6% of arrests in 2001 were for possession of drugs, not sale or manufacture according to *FBI UCR*, 2001.
[8] *Victimless Crime?* p.46.
[9] Ibid. p.47.

dislocation, the advent of mass communication and politicisation, and growing extremism – in short, Chaplin's 1936 film, *Modern Times*. The criminal law fell captive to a burgeoning intolerance armed with the repressive instrument of prohibition. Not content with the banning of alcohol, gambling and drugs, the legal moralist accomplished the closure of brothels not only in America but also throughout Europe during the first half of the century. Earlier, in the Middle Ages, the Protestant Reformation had achieved the same result by sweeping away the licensed brothels established by the Catholic Church. These were designed to exert a modicum of control over the incidence of venereal disease among the general population by at least curbing its spread by prostitution. Four hundred years later, the officially sanctioned brothels that existed in the major cities during the nineteenth century suffered a similar fate. These were centres of social and cultural resort providing gaming, dancing, wining and dining, cabaret and female companionship, and were frequented by local and international stars of stage and cinema and leading artists and intellectuals of the day. In an interesting documentary shown on SBS television,[10] entitled *The Paris Bordello*, containing extensive archival footage, it is clear that the female residents were well cared for and did not consider themselves victimised in any way, though they were subject to weekly medical examinations. Many of these bordellos even supplied free drinks and sex once a week for traumatised World War I veterans.

The Paris experience is particularly noteworthy as it incorporates all the significant features of the period. Taking advantage of a violent purge of collaborators during the German occupation, all these establishments were closed by one woman, a certain Marthe Richard, albeit with the moral support of Madame de Gaulle: a remarkable solo effort, even for the hand that rocks the cradle.

Notwithstanding the laudable mission statement contained in its purpose, namely 'for the protection of women', the law, in its banning of pimps and brothels and defining the latter as 'premises occupied by more than one prostitute' was designed to render the occupation as sordid and dangerous as possible. Denied a male protector, a safe working environment, the opportunity to share

---

[10] 19 March 2004.

the cost of accommodation or, indeed, to find any accommodation at all because of the risk to those responsible for premises of being charged with the offence of 'living off immoral earnings', the resultant streetwalker plies a solitary trade in isolated, run-down locations. 'Cooperation' with the police is essential because not only do the forces of law and order keep a record of the identity and location of every prostitute working in their precinct, but with no harm done and therefore no victim or complainant, arrest can be entirely arbitrary and discriminatory. Furthermore, the prostitute's all too frequent fate, often at the hands of serial killers, such as the national disgrace of the recent killing fields of Vancouver and Seattle, where respectively, Picton was credited with dispatching as many as fifty of these women and Ridgeway confessed to strangling forty-eight, serves as a constant reminder of the perils attendant upon their enforced vulnerability. Presumably, a missing prostitute is not regarded as a missing person.

Prostitutes commonly regard their services as providing an important safety valve, a view amply borne out by the current situation where, after centuries of repression, trafficking in women for sexual purposes is a major source of income for international crime syndicates. Presumably, Anglo-American jurisdictions consider this a price worth paying. Riding roughshod over the distinction between public indecency and private immorality in the interest of 'sexual empowerment', the law tolerates the 'sex industry' activities of the adult entertainment business, which is notorious for behaviour calculated to tease and tantalise, while continuing to condemn prostitution. Where else but in our culture does one find shameless public displays of hard-core pornography and strippers gyrating on bar counters inviting revellers to insert dollar bills in their vaginas,[11] while the private world of 'sex services' languishes in the sleazy twilight created by forbidden fruit, draconian legislation, sporadic policing and violent death?

Both St Augustine and later Thomas Aquinas conceded that prostitution was a necessary requirement of the human condition, the latter likening it to the plumbing of the palace. Subsequent

---

[11] Available in Washington DC.

apologists have hastened to translate their view into the concept of 'necessary evil', which is a contradiction in terms since anything that is necessary must have some value. The hypocrisy of using and at the same time shunning which is inherent in the concept is the subject of one of Guy de Maupassant's most successful short stories, *Boule de Suif*, the tale of a group of women travelling by coach. Stopped at a military checkpoint by a German officer demanding sexual favours before allowing them to proceed, they prevail upon one of their number to accede to the demand and then ostracize her for the rest of the journey.

Marvellously, in the topsy-turvy world of the legal moralist the very same outcomes of criminalising prostitution are served up as justifications for doing so! With staggering aplomb, we are warned that:

> ...if prostitution is not controlled it will become clandestine and this will lead to a loss of control over the criminal culture surrounding it and the spread of disease; it is the business of government, via the criminal law, to regulate morality, and prohibiting an activity enhances such regulation; the prostitute will lose out with regard to those humanistic concerns for her outcast condition if the trade is not proscribed and punished![12]

Equally strong in its opposition to legalisation, and ignoring legitimate concerns that it is her stigmatised condition which renders the prostitute a target of violence and corruption, feminist fundamentalism finds a voice in Susan Brownmiller. After affirming the view that legalising prostitution institutionalises the attitude that sex is a 'female service' affording that 'divine right' of the male 'to gain access to the female body', Brownmiller asserts that the creation of 'a cooperating class of women set aside ... and licensed for the purpose, is part and parcel of the mass psychology of rape.'[13] Fortunately, a somewhat higher standard of intellectual rigour is forthcoming in the arguments put forward by the group set up by the United Nations in 1959 to consider decriminalisation, and which persuaded it to recommend the removal of prostitution from the concerns of the criminal law.

---

[12] A miscellany of views taken from *Victimless Crime?* pp.57–8.

[13] Taken from *Victimless Crime?* p.58.

These included:

> ...a sensible acknowledgement that after centuries of prohibition the law had failed to eliminate it; illicit sexual activity has many gradations and the attempt to isolate one form from another was arbitrary and drove that selected into the arms of underworld organisations; criminalisation was an unwarranted invasion of the privacy of those indulging in a consensual activity, promoting unacceptable behaviour on the part of the police, and hampering those engaged in the trade, who wished to abandon it, from finding other employment.[14]

Some small justification for the law's excesses would be the knowledge that criminalisation has some influence on moral judgments, but there is no evidence of such a redeeming feature. What is or is not considered to be acceptable behaviour depends on incremental changes in values brought about by morally neutral developments, and not upon the dictates of the criminal law which, in any event, are no more than a matter of conjecture by those not directly involved in the activity in question. Indeed, Hart directs our attention to experiments which reveal a complete absence of any association between knowledge of the law and moral attitudes.[15]

The origin of harmless criminality is not difficult to find. Our history comes to us through the eyes of Christianity. Our perspective is that of the Christian Church. Our story is the tale of that one religion and it tells us that its arrival marks the dawn of civilisation.[16] Our previous existence was a heathen and brutish time, predictably referred to as the Dark Ages. Evidence that the 'barbarian hordes' which engulfed Rome carried with them articles for the cleaning of fingernails and the removal of nasal hair is studiously ignored.

Pagan England, which was wont to celebrate the sexual prowess of its deities, found it difficult to adjust to an immaculate conception and virgin birth, and, in quick time, was in dire need

---

[14] Taken from *Victimless Crime*, p.59.
[15] *The Morality of the Criminal Law*, p.44.
[16] Typical is the presentation in the volume entitled *Anglo-Saxon England*, in the *Oxford History of England*, Oxford, Clarendon Press, 1971.

of salvation. Celibacy became the ideal lifestyle, for sexual desire had been implanted by the Devil. The sexual act was made shameful and dirty, available only within Christian marriage, and then solely for the purpose of procreation. All the pleasures of the flesh were demonised and merited the fires of hell. These, however, were not always postponed as, along with heretics, women were roasted alive for having carnal knowledge of the Evil One whose physical presence among us forms a significant part of ecclesiastical doctrine. Evangelicals justify their existence by warning of this presence and employ experts, armed with various religious paraphernalia, to exorcise those possessed. Three years ago a mother in New South Wales, Australia, was charged before the Supreme Court with the murder of her nine-year-old daughter, Megan, on the day she was due to leave for boarding school, in the belief that she was evil and possessed of the Devil. Was her defence that of religious teaching? It seems not. Conviction followed upon a finding of mental illness causing such a delusion.[17]

Religious fundamentalism, exhorting the mortification of the flesh, has inflicted incalculable damage on that essential unity of the spiritual and the physical, and is responsible for much of the deplorable sexual behaviour afflicting society. It was not until Jane Austen's day that marriage became viewed as a sexual union expressing mutual respect and affection, and to this day 'clean living' means a celibate existence, and any reference to sexuality in Christ is blasphemy.[18]

Initiated by the Catholic Church, extremism disfigured the Protestant Reformation, which reached American shores in the seventeenth century, apparently refreshed by the sea voyage, and continues to be fuelled by modern evangelical movements. Some look back horrified by the excesses of Protestant zeal recounted by Hoskins in *Law and Authority in Early Massachusetts*,[19] where neighbour snooped on neighbour and fornicators, card players, dancers, adulterers, those in breach of the Sabbath and children

---

[17] *The Daily Telegraph*, 4 June 2002.
[18] *Lemon v Gay News* [1979] AC 617.
[19] George L Hoskins, New York, Macmillan, 1960, referred to by Ball and Friedman in *White-Collar Crime*, the Free Press, 1977, p.334.

disobedient towards parents were prosecuted in the courts. Writing in 1969, Hart observes:

> In America a glance at the penal statutes of the various states of the Union reveals something quite astonishing to English eyes. For in addition to such offences as are punishable under English law, there seems to be no sexual practice, except 'normal' relations between husband and wife and solitary acts of masturbation, which is not forbidden by the law of some state.[20]

He then goes on to point out that in the majority of states both fornication, not punishable in most of the civilised world, and adultery, not criminal since Cromwell's time, still attract criminal sanctions. Such evidence tends to confirm the view that freedom, in its true sense of a liberty to indulge unpopular activities that do no discernible harm to others, has not flourished in American soil.

Concern has been expressed recently that heterosexual congress, as distinct from a growing eagerness to discuss and display it, is in decline in the United States. Celibacy, it is said, is staging a comeback – within marriage;[21] and sperm banks, now a thriving industry, cater for women with maternal leanings who merely select off the shelf an anonymous father advertising his stature, race, colour of eyes and intellectual ability, thereby avoiding the hassle of a relationship or a man about the house. The love scene, once a staple of earlier Hollywood film-makers reflecting a mutual tenderness, has been supplanted on our screens by an Attenborough-like episode of frenzied rutting and grunting. The shared experience of the dance has given way to the individualistic romp of the disco, explained by some as a bonding with the tribe. Entertainment is sought in topless service, strippers and lap dancers. We have come a long way in three score years and ten from Fred Astaire and Ginger Rogers, 'Dancing Cheek to Cheek'.

Writing on the American scene, Auberon Waugh[22] referred to the soaring rates of suicide, many more teenagers dying by their own hand than by homicide and the grotesque prosecution of

---

[20] *Law, Liberty and Morality*, p.26.
[21] Spectrum, *Weekend Sydney Morning Herald*, 22 February 2003.
[22] *The Sunday Telegraph* (UK), 25 October 1998.

female 'rapists', that is, those having intercourse with underage males, one of whom, having fallen pregnant twice by her fifteen-year-old lover (on the second occasion during a brief release from prison, where the first child was born) faces the possibility of life imprisonment. He offered the opinion that the oddest thing about Americans is their attitude to sex, and that the continued persecution of these females 'in this woman-dominated society suggests a repudiation of any sort of heterosexual activity at all. It would seem that the women have given up on sex altogether, leaving men to watch porno videos.' Perhaps they are too busy with one in three children growing up under a single parent regime.

Despite these anxieties regarding America's moral health, Australia has not always shrugged off the influence of American agencies bent on pressing upon others their own dysfunctional policies. Before 1943, Australia maintained a regime of licensed drug use, implementing the view that drugs were a health problem and not a matter of criminality. Under this system the welfare and management of addicts was supervised by community-based medical practitioners. However, this approach was hastily abandoned in favour of prohibition under threat of withdrawal of American military cooperation. The heroin trials planned by the Australian Capital Territory a few years ago were abruptly halted following pressure from Washington and Vienna (the base of the American-dominated International Narcotics Control Board, or INCB) despite worldwide acknowledgement of Australia's success, through its harm immunisation programmes such as needle exchange, in controlling the spread of AIDS. In March 2000 the INCB charged Australia with violating international narcotics treaties by pursuing the planned safe injecting rooms.[23]

More remarkable is the success achieved by the more populous eastern states of Australia in curbing the police corruption, violence, exploitation by organised crime and disease habitually associated with prostitution, by legalising the second

---

[23] Much of this is taken from an article entitled 'Just Say No to America' by Dr Ernest Drucker, Professor of Epidemiology and Social Medicine, appearing in the *Sydney Morning Herald*, 6 March 2000.

oldest profession[24] and establishing a system of licensed brothels. Yet in 1999, and blithely ignoring the Biblical caution regarding the mote in one's own eye, the US State Department, in its country-by-country survey of human rights abuse, had the effrontery to allege that this enlightened policy was encouraging the international slave trade, citing anecdotal evidence of a traffic in women to work in sweatshops and an increasing number of children entering the country as sex slaves.[25]

It is well known that some brothel owners hark back to the good old days when the police supervised the sex trade and, being well able to afford 'kickbacks', were assured of less competition. In a two-page spread in the *Sydney Morning Herald* detailing the ownership and location of brothels in the Sydney region, this view, together with allegations that many such brothels are illegal, is given an uncritical hearing.[26] While it is essential to repudiate the fundamentalist belief that ends justify means, it is equally important that the present hard-won arrangement (the outcome of the Woods Royal Commission of 1995, which exposed massive police corruption connected with the trade) be sustained by stringent observance of the licensing regulations.

The growing concern about the trade in women for sexual purposes, now worldwide, is not matched by an understanding that its cause is the stubborn attitude towards prostitution. Those most vociferous in its condemnation appear not only to be bewildered by the discovery that the sex drive, like the pursuit of wealth, is 'universal and insatiable' (to use their words), but unaware that smuggling, which is not a recent phenomenon, requires an illegal product. Glanville Williams recounts the amusing tale of cross-Channel trippers 'attempting' to smuggle sugar, which was in short supply at the time, to illustrate the important difference between a legal and a mere factual impossibility. A more germane example would be a 'conspiracy' to commit adultery – though this, presumably, could still be charged in those pockets of medievalism in America to which Hart refers.

Obviously, countries like Australia, where in some states prosti-

---

[24] Lawyers are the oldest, since God gave the law to Adam.
[25] *Sydney Morning Herald*, 28 February 2000.
[26] *Sydney Morning Herald*, 30 August 1999.

tution has been legalised, will be a favoured destination for such women; but it must be remembered that trafficking in women is only a facet of the larger issue of illegal immigration, a malady with which countries enjoying superior living standards are increasingly plagued. The response must continue to be eternal vigilance on the part of the immigration authorities and, with Australia, strict enforcement of licensing controls and existing age limits. But this is small beer compared with the calamitous consequences flowing from banning the product or service itself.

What is unacceptable is that those jurisdictions which have created the problem by singling out for punishment only the downmarket sale of sex,[27] should avoid censure by shifting the blame to others who have not. This is the thinly disguised purpose of the recurring attacks (one as recent as 2003) by the US State Department levelled at Australia alleging responsibility for the burgeoning 'slave trade', under the somewhat incongruous banner of abuse of human rights; incongruous inasmuch as, however catholic the concept of human rights may be, it is difficult to accommodate within it the denial of personal liberty involved in prohibiting selected women from deriving some small financial advantage from their gender. There may well be advantages in the areas of trade and technology flowing from a more intimate relationship with the only world power, but Australia must be vigilant in preserving its own values, not those of a society recognised as moralistic, violent and racist.

Infused with the authority of Christendom, the legal moralist insists that the criminal sanction is an appropriate vehicle for the expression of moral condemnation. Exploited in turn by church, state and organised crime, the category of victimless crime has involved, at one time or another, fornication, masturbation, homosexuality, suicide, prostitution, gambling, adultery, abortion, drug use (including alcohol) and blasphemy.

Since they pose no threat to persons or property, they have been characterised as 'social problems' inimical to the pursuit of such daunting concepts as 'community values' and 'social hygiene'. Their persistent prosecution lends weight to the opinion of Mencken, who observed:

---

[27] The opinion of the United Nations quoted on p.35.

> The fundamental aim of practical politics is to keep the populace alarmed (and hence clamorous to be led to safety) by menacing it with an endless series of hobgoblins, all of them imaginary.[28]

In the meanwhile, real crime involving flesh and blood victims has become the poor relation both in public money and police effort as the forces of law and order track down drug users and the likes of Ms Brown and her benighted customers. It does not seem to be appreciated that over and above the shockingly criminogenic consequences of banning harmless activities, their prosecution violates that dominion or autonomy human beings require over their persons and private space. A society that does not pause at this threshold cannot be considered free.

The progress of this category has been uneven, even cyclical, as pressure groups and fresh outbursts of extremism temporarily hijack the legislative process. However, with a gradual recognition of the values of privacy and personal freedom, its content, over time, has diminished with the remarkable exception of prostitution and drug use; remarkable inasmuch as, with removal of the harmful outcomes of criminalisation, these are the least deserving of punishment. The reasons for this phenomenon must be examined, but there is evidence aplenty of the conflict theory at work: the social status (including ethnicity) of the practitioner, be they junkie or whore, being of far greater significance than the nature of the practice itself.

---

[28] Mencken, H L, *In Defence of Women*. Alfred A Knopf, 1922, p.23.

Prostitution and Drug Use

Prostitution

Whatever the perspective, be it the operation of market forces in a case where demand outstrips supply, the conflict between the competing interests of gender, or the capacity of the human race for self-deception and dishonesty, female prostitution continues to generate a mix of fascination and revulsion. This is evident in the inordinately large variety of language employed to describe both the female involved and the activity itself. Earlier versions of the latter, more judgmental than descriptive, or seeking to limit the practice to a chosen minority, employ terms such as promiscuous, indiscriminate, lewd, base, vile or common, but these are either standards impossible of measurement or mere pejorative comment. Perhaps to dispel any suggestion that it refers to social status, the much favoured epithet 'common prostitute' has received judicial mention. It has been held that the addition of 'common' differentiates the woman who prostitutes herself in a once-in-a-lifetime lapse from those who habitually indulge in the practice with all and sundry. So, we have it on legal authority that in the measurement of frequency more than once renders an event common. Putting to one side emotive surplusage, female prostitution can be defined as engaging in sexual activity with males who are not familiars, for financial reward. Removing the gender-based orientation but venturing upon uncharted seas with the inclusion of 'usually', the consultation document 'Paying the Price' issued by the Home Office in July 2004 defines prostitution as 'the exchange of sexual services for some form of payment – usually money or drugs.'

The continued criminality of both prostitution itself (as is the case in America) or the more common but equally drastic device of banning all the prerequisites for carrying on the trade, such as soliciting, pimping, advertising and brothel-keeping (the position in the UK) presents the justice system with a problem. This is because, apart from those pockets of medievalism which according to Hart still survive in the United States, the legalisation of fornication, that is, illicit or extramarital sexual intercourse, removes its criminal foundation. In short, if illicit sex is legal, how can selling it be illegal? Prostitution is simply a service, like any other to which we have become accustomed, such as legal advice, hairdressing and those provided by places of entertainment. Solicitation is the same as the activities of any street trader, and keeping a brothel is no different, legally, than having chambers occupied by more than one barrister. As has been pointed out more than once, the act of simply selling a service or offering it for sale cannot convert that service into a criminal activity. In the words of Mill, 'the fact of following anything as an occupation, and living or profiting by the practice of it, cannot make that criminal which would otherwise be admissible.'[1]

The employment of vacuous and emotive expressions such as 'the commercialisation of vice' cannot cloak the difficulty or disguise the fact that fornication (presumably the 'vice' referred to) is no longer criminal. Various strategies, for example drawing the distinction, dubious at the best of times, between what is unlawful and what is criminal, favoured by some feminists, is unhelpful since fornication is neither. The widespread use of the charge 'offences connected with prostitution' fares no better unless it is a genuine reference to a situation where a lawful provider is in breach of regulations imposed upon the trade, such as a publican supplying alcohol after hours or to minors. This is plainly not the case. Fleiss was sentenced to three years' imprisonment for procuring, but such a charge would prevent any business from recruiting staff. The gravamen of the charge against Ms Brown was public indecency, but parked vehicles are a favoured location for courting couples left unmolested by the police. Clearly, the blanket bans on advertising (Shaw v DPP, supra) and soliciting would seriously hamper high street shopping, bearing in mind that, with regard to the latter, the offence is to solicit a man in the street, and has been interpreted by a

---

[1] *On Liberty*, 1859, at p.232.

censorious judiciary as not requiring the presence of the woman in the street at all provided the man is, nor that any approach or communication occur.

It is arguable, therefore, that the legal basis for prosecution is at least open to question, but there is no doubt that the nature of its enforcement, being entirely discretionary, is, by definition, unlawful. Designed merely to 'keep it under wraps', the criminal law has created an unedifying police playground of 'soft targets', bestowing flattering crime statistics, and involving unsavoury features inconceivable in any other context than that of a voiceless minority at the very bottom of the pecking order. Indeed, it is readily acknowledged, for example in the consultation paper just mentioned, that the control mechanism most favoured consists of an unscrupulous mix of toleration interspersed with periodic arrest and occasional sweeping crackdowns – quite simply, a climate wherein the rule of law has ceased to exist.

If, as we are led to believe, prostitution threatens the foundation of society, likened by Lord Devlin to treason, how is it that it is allowed, subject to police supervision, as to both occurrence and location? Evidence of this phenomenon is found in the current existence of so-called 'managed tolerance zones' (the 'red light' districts of saner, less extreme times), but even these have been condemned, incongruously enough, by those reduced to the vestigial complaint that the harm done by prostitution, and the factor which justifies the imposition of criminal sanctions, is that of nuisance. It is inconceivable that a similar approach could be adopted towards other dangers such as those posed by property damage and physical violence. A partial explanation on offer is that the criminal justice system makes extensive use of prostitutes to inform on the criminal underworld into which they have been forced.

The condition of the prostitute is an extreme example of status degradation. The crucial differential in prosecution is not the commonplace nature of the act but the reputation of the woman who performs it. Furthermore, Anglo-American law has always adopted the policy that any offence committed is committed by the female partner alone. This discriminatory rule has led to scandalous abuse. For example, in South Africa during the apartheid era it was for some years officially sanctioned policy for police officers, in plain clothes and in pairs, to visit prostitutes and, immediately after completion of the service, arrest the woman involved. Unwelcome publicity ensued when a short article appeared in a Johannesburg newspaper, entitled 'Our Sexy Policemen', giving details of these operations, including the collection of items of female underwear as trophies of such tours of duty, and the practice was hastily abandoned. There was no public outcry, no police inquiry, no investigation of a possible involvement by the courts; merely a brief statement by the then Minister of Justice, C R Swart, that the method employed 'had caused too much trouble'. This type of behaviour is now a thing of the past, with a new dispensation ushering in establishments euphemistically termed 'ranches', accompanied by the usual protests from women's groups, previously silent about the earlier undercover operations, but now vociferous in their disapproval, uttering the familiar mantra that 'it is this kind of thing which is destroying our society.'

English television has documented similar excursions to massage parlours in the UK where, during a sampling of the advertised attractions, a female operative may be induced to offer sexual intercourse, thereby providing unambiguous evidence to support a prosecution for keeping a brothel, a crime carrying terms of imprisonment.

In a singular approach, Sweden has shunted the long-standing discriminatory rule into reverse. In terms of the Swedish experiment, it is now the *male* who solicits or pays for sex who alone commits the offence; the female who trades sex for reward, or solicits for the purpose of prostitution, no longer acts illegally. This affords the opportunity for role reversal, with the female in a position to blackmail or arrange arrest after the event. Sweden has thus regressed, joining the ranks of those few remaining Western countries, such as America, where prostitution itself, irrespective of any public manifestation, is a criminal activity, but curiously enough, only for the occasional male customer.

Legally marginalised and uniquely identified solely by occupation, the prostitute finds that the law inflicts upon her a degree of social segregation second only to the denial of human rights occasioned by incarceration in a prison cell, through the device of exposing all those who would supply her with refreshment, entertainment and lodging to the risk of criminal prosecution.[2] Little wonder, then, that many develop a drug problem which, with a cynicism to which we have grown accustomed, is used to justify more of the same. According to coverage by English television, prostitutes have been turned away by international aid agencies. Just such a woman refused help during the Bosnian upheavals, and arrested by police for protesting such treatment, appreciated the irony of her situation, pointing out, when later interviewed, that her kind were the only ones who had *not* practised ethnic discrimination. On a more recent ABC programme,[3] a sympathetic interviewer listened as a convicted drug courier complained bitterly that on her arrest she had been incarcerated 'with prostitutes and junkies', seemingly oblivious to the fact that these were the very victims of her trade in misery and death. It is common knowledge that in America on a jocular night out a posse of police will conduct a round-up of prostitutes who have ventured out of doors, load them in the wagon and, transporting them miles out of town, leave them to find their own way back. Obviously, the frontier spirit is still alive and well.

The reasons for this outlawed condition implicate both genders and society itself, and explains the lack of interest in and trivialisation of male prostitution. The prostitute, who guarantees low cost sexual release without commitment or subsequent complaint,[4] is perceived as a threat to the female who, biologically programmed, requires the security of a lasting relationship within which to rear her progeny. For the macho male, driven by the evolutionary imperative to spread his seed, 'paying for it' is humiliating, a subject of unrelenting scorn by male and female alike – more so because, in large measure, the prostitute caters for those unattractive, old and even disabled members of the sex. As for society, how it sees itself is largely, but not exclusively, derived from myth and legend. Even religious, biological or patriarchal

---

[2] See the wealth of legislation detailed in *Rook and Ward on Sexual Offences,* second edition, Sweet and Maxwell, 1977, Chapter 9.

[3] ABC (Australia), 20 July 2000.

[4] See Kinsey, op. cit. p.29.

factors may explain the phenomenon that communities invariably evince a parochial, if not proprietorial, interest in the position and behaviour of their women.

Parochialism often seeks to lay the blame on foreigners and immigrants, and there is regular application of double standards. From earliest times the Hebrews warned of the menace of 'pagan harlots' and the current targets of the growth in international trafficking in drugs and women are the Romanians, Slavs, Thais, Colombians and Hispanics. On the home front during the 1939–1945 war, the position of the American matron was assured by a regime inflicting criminal sanctions on all sexual activity outside marriage, but matters were different in foreign parts. The armed forces overseas were catered for by locally recruited women procured by the US government and paid in American dollars. The service provided fell far short of that offered by Heidi Fleiss. Anecdotal evidence has it that there were long queues at the recreational booths, often in oppressive weather, and the time allotted each doughboy of three minutes from entry to exit (of the booth) seems miserly after a long wait. These arrangements were recorded at the time in a hit single by the Andrews Sisters entitled, 'Rum and Coca-Cola'.

Prostitution has entirely missed out on the liberalising process which has gradually eliminated so much victimless crime, even though it is, arguably, the most innocuous of all the offences in the category. This recalcitrance on the part of the Anglo-American system is unmoved by the evidence available from those countries where it has been legalised, revealing the trade operating in a safe and virtually crime-free environment without a trace of that moral decay prophesied by the legal moralist. Such communities continue to wonder what all the fuss is about. However, enlightenment may still be imperilled by the offerings of some Australian television. Recently the hitherto reputable SBS, in its 9.30 p.m. news bulletin, succumbed to temptation.[5] Its brief coverage of the significant decriminalisation of prostitution, by the narrowest of margins, in New Zealand was laced, not with an account of views expressed in the debate, but with images of leggy females, stiletto-heeled and micro-skirted, framed against

---

[5] 26 June 2003.

the obligatory background of the 'red light' district with the ubiquitous cigarette dangling from scarlet mouth or scarlet fingernails. The only absentee, presumably engaged on other television assignments, was Satan himself. Nevertheless, the ABC's Friday night *Stateline* retains prime position with its treatment of an application for a brothel licence in New South Wales, wherein the cast consisted entirely of well-rounded bottoms. If this editorial output passes for intelligent coverage, then our Christian heritage continues to thwart the coming of age in this youngest recruit to the media.

The prostitute has not benefited from militant marches such as those accompanying the campaign for Gay Rights, nor have prominent writers and personalities raised their voices in protest, though a number of actresses have achieved stardom playing the role of the hooker. However, the most damaging factor is undoubtedly that, unlike the issue of abortion, which for many takes human life, the cause of the lowly whore has not been espoused by feminism.

At first blush, it is difficult to understand an interpretation of emancipation which advocates the right of a woman to destroy the foetus in her womb and yet denies a right to make harmless use of her own body. However, taking into account the avowed hostility directed at perceived male domination, it is hardly likely that such a movement would take kindly to those of its sisterhood who let the side down by catering for male lust when, in its view, the entire heterosexual experience is just another example of male exploitation and subjugation of women. Indeed, as is evident from media comment, the indestructibility of the trade continues to rankle. An example is the treatment accorded a Canadian programme aired on SBS television[6] focusing on the artistic creativity and sexual freedom enjoyed during the 1920s and 1930s in Paris and Berlin, cities predictably favoured by expatriate Americans such as Hemingway, Joyce, Cole Porter and Picasso. In a preview quite out of keeping with the balanced tenor of the series, Clare Morgan succumbs to that ribaldry habitually associated with any reference to prostitution and remarks:

---

[6] 14 January 2005.

> With the old world order swept aside, Berlin in the 1920s was the metropolis of vice, with more strip clubs, gay joints, knocking shops and wobbly bits than you could poke a whore's drawers at.[7]

Similarly, in a preview of the final episode of a remarkably non-judgmental American series, again shown on SBS television,[8] on the daily lives of the women working in two of Nevada's legal brothels, Lisa Prior abandons professional detachment and writes:

> The access the documentary makers have to these women's lives is extraordinary but one criticism that must be made is there is not much focus on the clients. That means you get the impression that all the women do all day is chat in the bar, collect towels from reception and have showers, rather than the grimmer, sweatier, uglier reality.[9]

The uninitiated are left wondering what this 'uglier reality' is, over and above normal heterosexual congress.

Finally, and also as a reminder of the time when New South Wales was comfortable with the control of prostitution as a police perk (the regimen still current in other Anglo-American jurisdictions except neighbouring Queensland, Victoria and New Zealand), we learn from a piece in the *Sydney Morning Herald*[10] that the graffiti carved into the cedar wood furnishings of Darlington's criminal courts is to be heritage listed. These courts, reputed to be the longest continuously running criminal courts in the world, have, over the years, witnessed much of the drama of the human predicament played out before legal luminaries, cub reporters and a prurient public. One of these, Blanche D'Alpuget, a reporter for the *Daily Mirror*, a now defunct Sydney newspaper, describes her attendance there as 'a marvellous education', recalling that 'Monday mornings were spent watching parades of prostitutes arrested at the weekend.'

Faced with the intractability of the supply, feminism has shifted its focus to the demand side of the trade and has been

---

[7] 'The Guide', *Sydney Morning Herald*, 10–16 January 2005.
[8] 17 December 2004.
[9] 'The Guide', *Sydney Morning Herald*, 13–19 December 2004.
[10] 6 September 2004.

instrumental in intensifying and enlarging the campaign against prostitution by including a new quarry, the hitherto immune male customer. Such a push against the customer as well as the supplier is of great significance, as it is contrary to previous criminal justice policy. This aspect will be examined later,[11] but meanwhile it is obvious that it dramatically extends the reach of the criminal law. Already this is evident, as police activity increasingly targets the soliciting male client who now makes up more than 40% of those arrested. Trapping operatives have also welcomed this new dawn by mounting individual and large-scale exercises. Cruising late-night bars, female police officers, suitably attired, invite solicitation from solitary males.

One of the sights of Washington DC at night is a brightly lit arena where the ladies of the town disport themselves under the watchful eye of cohorts of police playing cat and mouse with circling male clients whose names, if booked, are listed next day in the morning newspaper. Similar events are staged in other cities, constituting open-air theatre – American-style. A noteworthy scalp of similar sporting activities, if less flamboyant, conducted in the vicinity of King's Cross station in London, was that of the Director of Public Prosecutions himself, leading to the ruin of a career and the subsequent suicide of his wife.

Drugs

As far as is known, the human race has always indulged in drug use. From earliest times, and for purposes which have remained unchanged, the habit has been a feature of mankind's lifestyle, ranging from potion to prescription. Taken to satisfy a lifetime of requirements – physical, psychological and emotional – they have provided for sickness, injury, relaxation, recreation, a sense of well-being, a desire for longevity and have been taken on a host of social and religious occasions. That some drug takers harm themselves and, inadvertently, others, is seemingly as unavoidable as other calamities, such as the death toll on our roads and environmental pollution; but we do not ban the motor vehicle or the means of production, we merely subject them to regulation.

---

[11] On pp.52–53.

Prohibition and punishment cannot cure addiction. The question is, can they prevent it? This is the stated goal of the so-called 'war on drugs' which has been waged throughout the twentieth century and now takes up the lion's share of all police operations. It is estimated that in America the cost is US$75 billion per year.[12] This 'war' is also credited with corrupting entire police forces, like the LAPD in the late 1990s, and with unprecedented increases in secondary crime to feed the habit and the incidence of the habit itself. International drug cartels now control a multi-billion dollar enterprise which dictates the supply, quality and price of the product. How has this been achieved in so short a space of time?

To draw liberally from the account by Meier and Geis,[13] throughout the nineteenth century drugs which are now banned were freely available over the counter in the form of patent medicines. Opium and its derivatives, such as morphine and heroin, were widely used for 'female disorders' and as cough remedies, and cocaine was regularly added to wine products. The 1897 edition of the Sears and Roebuck catalogue advertised hypodermic kits priced at $1.50, and we are all conversant with the drug habit of the celebrated fictional character of Sherlock Holmes.

All this changed during the succeeding century as the criminal law blundered into a campaign motivated by a desire to regulate, and thereby tax, the manufacture and sale of products containing heroin and cocaine and to prevent their use by ethnic minorities. The recreational use of marijuana amongst middle-class white Americans was of no concern, but its spread, via migrant workers, to African Americans concentrated in the large cities, combined with its use by black jazz musicians, perceived as a focus of teenage rebellion, ensured its criminalisation. The essential fear factor was readily supplied by the moguls of the media, and society was assailed by images of rampaging, mind-blown black youths and opium dens wherein unspeakable defilements were perpetrated by Orientals upon white virgins.

'The racist motivation,' write Meier and Geis 'of this early legislation is unmistakable, as is the fear generated by certain

---

[12] *Victimless Crime?* at p.108.
[13] Ibid at pp.87–9.

drugs. Throughout the twentieth century, it has been the characteristics of users, not those of the drugs, that have been the better predictors of drug laws.'[14]

History, it is said, repeats itself. The foolishness of Canute's admirers has rubbed off on America's ONDCP (Office of National Drug Control Policy), and nothing has been learned from the unmitigated disaster of the Prohibition years. This debilitating experience in American history is now no more than the subject of bouts of voyeuristic viewing of mobsters and tommy guns akin to the widespread fascination with the exploits of Jack the Ripper. Jack, however, is now small fry compared with the body count of those more recently availing themselves of a deliberate policy of defencelessness imposed upon the prostitute, and which certainly reduces their number.[15]

What astonishes about these spells of retrospection is the absence of hindsight – no sense of having been there before, no realisation that the intervention of the criminal law in the campaign against drugs is but another fruitless exercise, this time of catastrophic proportions, utterly dwarfing in both scale and consequences a previous visit within living memory.

In a futile attempt to circumvent the law of supply and demand and justify its punishment of harmless transgressors, the criminal law upends the rule that demand fuels supply and demonises the supplier. This stratagem, which is evident throughout the realm of victimless crime, portrays the ordinary citizen as an unwilling victim seduced by satanic forces, thereby downgrading the demand as a passing frailty and rendering the banned activity suitably susceptible to criminal coercion. This gross misrepresentation of the true state of affairs has stifled the development of effective demand-reduction measures based on social disapproval and awareness of the risks involved. Vast sums of money have been diverted away from shoring up the coastal defences with community-based health projects, educational programmes, advertising campaigns and the enlistment of high-profile role models, especially sports stars, in a forlorn attempt, via

---

[14] Ibid. at p.90.
[15] For example, the Yorkshire Ripper and, already mentioned, Vancouver's Picton and Ridgeway of Seattle.

vice squads, to stop the tide coming in. Billions of dollars have been spent on criminalising addiction, a condition frequently caused by low self-esteem; yet it is obvious that the stigma of criminality does not enhance self-respect.

It is in this context that the Swedish experiment, presently confined to prostitution, must be considered. Displaying imprudent confidence in the efficacy of the penal sanction to achieve demand reduction, it envisages massive intervention by the criminal law through exclusive concentration on the more abundant customer – leaving the more limited supplier exonerated. Logically, there is no reason why this approach should not be applied across the entire spectrum of harmless criminality, exposing, for example, the post-abortion mother to prosecution and punishment, not the abortionist; the player rather than the gambling syndicate; the user rather than the trafficking cartel. But would we have the police and penitentiary capacity to service this brave new world?

A first step in the effort to end prohibition has to be decriminalisation, which requires political will and some faith in the resilience of the human race. Fortunately, there is a viable model to hand. The controlled availability of alcohol and tobacco, substances equally harmful and, in the case of the former, more dangerous than the most damaging of banned drugs, is a success story worth repeating. Admittedly, lives continue to be ruined by these products, and there is the occasional break-in at local stores and even instances of smuggling by weekend trippers where price discrepancies exist; but nevertheless, society has escaped relatively unscathed compared with the calamity visited upon us by the drugs war. There will always be zealots who demand more of the same, and legal moralists undeterred by the fact that the dire predictions of those of their kind never materialise. However, other, Continental, jurisdictions have already decriminalised with encouraging results, and minor parties in the UK and Australia have called for it.

Decriminalisation is, however, not enough. Indeed, legalisation without an end to illicit supply would be a recipe for disaster. To achieve elimination of the illegal trade, current demand must be met through the manufacture and sale, under government supervision, of presently banned substances at an affordable price, as is done with alcohol and tobacco. It is estimated that one gram of pharmacy heroin costs four cents, whereas an equivalent amount of uncertain quality on the black market fetches US$70, the difference being accounted for by hazardous access, unpredictable shortages and unconscionable profit. Under the existing punitive regime, every major drug bust is good news for the cartels, in whose hands supporters of prohibition seem content to leave exclusive supply, whereas the substantial revenues generated by controlled provision would be available to tackle addiction for what it is, namely, a health problem.

The timid would no doubt urge availability by prescription only, and this has been suggested as a possible first step, but in the long run it could be self-defeating. It is the taboo surrounding drugs, and the image that their use is chic and sophisticated, and not a foolish demonstration of youthful rebellion, that is so much a part of the problem. What is required is political *will*, not political *interference*. It is a commonly held view, at least among health care professionals, that better health service delivery and clinical outcomes occur when there is a minimum of political interference.[16]

---

[16] See generally, 'Illicit Drugs Policy', a policy document issued by the Royal Australasian College of Physicians, the Royal Australian and New Zealand College of Psychiatrists, and GROW, 2004.

White-Collar Crime

Definition

White-collar crime has been variously described, but, escaping the lack of certainty surrounding the definition of crime in general, this category of criminality lends itself to comparatively precise identification. It consists of deceptive behaviour causing harm, usually, but not exclusively, of a financial nature, by persons of upper socio-economic status taking advantage of the opportunities presented by their occupation. A simple example would be that of a company director publishing false information regarding the company's finances, leading to financial loss by investors, or a medical practitioner colluding with a pharmacist to cause loss to a health authority by claiming false prescription charges. The latter, however, may also place at risk patients cared for by the authority by depriving it, through reducing the public purse, of necessary equipment and expertise.[1]

The category represents a departure from the familiar one-on-one model of crime, which has constituted the main focus of prosecution, because its victims are numerous and diffuse. By contrast with harmless criminality, it is always predatory and, unlike much violent crime which results from emotional outbursts, it is always premeditated: the outcome of a rational choice based on a calculated appraisal of risk and benefit. Finally, the relationship between offender and victim is impersonal, the *mens rea* (state of mind of the offender) being, in the Continental idiom, *dolus generalis* (general or indiscriminate intention), the same as that of the terrorist bomber who is unconcerned as to the identity of his or her victims.

---

[1] According to a report in *The Sunday Times* (UK) of 20 April 1997, this practice is widespread and costs the National Health Service more than £200 million a year.

Problems with Pursuing White-Collar Crime

Most, if not all, of the difficulties encountered by the criminal justice system in carrying out its rightful role as vanguard in the battle against white-collar crime have been self-inflicted.

A major obstacle is the adversarial system of trial itself. This is a method of trial in which skilled and experienced champions do battle before a judicial officer, and in some cases, a jury,[2] and is typical of the Anglo-American confrontational approach to dispute resolution. Its supporters believe that only out of the dust of conflict will the true facts emerge and the merits prevail. There are, however, a number of factors which militate against this desirable outcome. The fact that it is viewed as a contest places undue weight on the performance of the champion (counsel), whose professionalism dictates that the issue of innocence or guilt is equated with the verdict of the court. This occupational requirement has led to much unkind comment such as that expressed by Professor Appelbaum of the Department of Ethics at Harvard that lawyers as a class 'might accurately be described as serial liars because they repeatedly try to induce others to believe in the truth of propositions or in the validity of arguments that they believe to be false.'[3] Whether or not such behaviour amounts to outright lying, it would be unacceptable in the larger community. This issue of the existence of abnormal ethical regimes within circumscribed occupations is adverted to later.

This form of trial takes little or no account of the raw material before the court, be it the accused, complainant or witness or, of course, the jury. An important instrument in the forensic armour on display is the art of cross-examination which, in the hands of a skilled practitioner, is considered to be the 'most effective weapon for truth ever forged.' Unhappily, very little in life can be accommodated within a simple 'yes' or 'no' rejoinder to a carefully crafted question, not necessarily designed to reveal the truth.[4] The fabled conscientious traveller on the Clapham

---

[2] This is the standard composition of the forum which varies, however, depending on its status in the hierarchy and the seriousness of the offence.
[3] Quoted in 'Insight', *Sydney Morning Herald*, 11 June 2001, p.15.
[4] See Russell Fox QC, quoted ibid.

omnibus or, in more sophisticated times, the package holiday-maker, tends to be maddeningly circuitous in expression, irritatingly discursive and unforgivably irrelevant.

Standing alone in the witness box, exposed to much intimidatory theatre (for the benefit of the public gallery, now enlarged by television), and long after the event, those subjected to this inquisition become certain of only one thing – the desire to escape. It is hardly surprising that the accused at least is given the right to refuse such an ordeal.

The reliance upon oral testimony given in open court as a method of eliciting the facts may have been unavoidable in times past before the advent of widespread literacy, but is hardly appropriate in cases where the evidence lies in the documentation of a computerised age. In any event, a preference for this survivor of the oral tradition over the printed word affronts common experience, as memory and recall are notoriously untrustworthy. No more than twenty-four hours after an event, our traumatised recollection of precisely what occurred is lost, submerged in all manner of internal and external influences. The so-called 'eyewitness' is choice fare for the seasoned campaigner. Under lengthy cross-examination, the honest witness testifying months afterwards is easily persuaded that they are not sure about anything that transpired at the scene except perhaps their presence. For the purposes of defence counsel, the printed word lacks the drama and susceptibility of the witness at the scene of the crime.

Opinions differ regarding the merits of the concomitant feature of trial by jury. The stuff of folklore, ensuring that prince and pauper receive equal treatment under law, this time-honoured English institution has been the subject of much fulsome praise by both bench and bar. Variously described as 'part of the history of England'[5] a 'palladium of justice'[6] constituting 'the finest way of judging innocence or guilt',[7] its frailties are, nevertheless, cruelly apparent when dealing with white-collar crime. Exposed

---

[5] Sir Travers Humphreys, quoted in Glanville Williams, *The Proof of Guilt*, Steven and Sons, 1963, p.287.
[6] Sir William Blackstone, quoted ibid, p.288.
[7] Baroness Kennedy QC, *The Daily Telegraph* (UK), 21 January 2000, p.14.

to the unfamiliar environment of corporate finance and its membership weakened by both generous exemptions for the better educated and lack of experience (the sole qualification for service), it is obliged to listen, sometimes for months on end, to accounting-speak without provision even for the taking of notes.

The entire production, part medieval pageant, part morality play, is hugely expensive in time, money and other resources. Designed to deal with the illiterate miscreant charged with the familiar sins, it finds itself thrust into reverse. The jury is wrong-footed in carrying out its legendary role as defender of the lowly against establishment power, and the legal profession is put out of countenance by the prospect of members of the upper socio-economic class being included within the criminal fraternity and acquiring a criminal record. Indeed, it is mortified by the possibility that the respectable and well educated, like themselves, could be put behind bars with street people. If all else fails, defence counsel will summon up consultants to give expert opinion that their client, condemned to imprisonment, is in the last stages of a life-threatening illness or advanced dementia. Their heart-warming recovery once the threat of a prison cell is removed is further testimony to the efficacy of the 'justice game' – a borrowing from Geoffrey Robertson, the Australian-born human rights lawyer, author and academic.

Traditional crime is apparent and calls for a reactive response. On the other hand, and for different reasons, both harmless criminality and white-collar crime suffer low visibility and require proactive measures such as surveillance, undercover operations, 'stings', wire taps and raids. These have been vigorously employed in the detection of the former, whereas in the pursuit of the latter they are conspicuously absent. It seems that such activities raise insuperable difficulties involving civil rights when the target is not a drug addict or prostitute, but a corporate executive or politician. One explanation offered for the 'dragging of feet' by the system is the scale and complexity of much of the fraud involved. As Levi remarks, 'The regulation of fraud is a messy business'[8] – as messy as the plethora of governmental and quasi-governmental agencies,

---

[8] *White-Collar Crime Reconsidered*, ed. Schlegel and Weisburd, Northeastern University Press, Boston, 1992, p.171.

(manifestly ineffective and chronically undermanned and under-funded) currently dedicated to its control. Geographical and jurisdictional difficulties, inherent in tracking mobile, white-collar miscreants and, in a computerised age, the missing and even more mobile funds, are obvious, with the demoralising outcome that the success rate is much higher with localised low-level activity. For example, in the 1990s the FBI tripled the number of agents assigned to investigate employee theft and welfare fraud, with the result that the number of prosecutions for these relatively minor transgressions increased by 60%. Surely, however, elevation of the focus of police activity above street level, coupled with appropriate training and the necessary political will, would bring similar but more significant rewards. Instead of concentrating their effort on penetrating the ranks of *organised* crime, the forces of law and order could try trawling the corporate suites of *organisational* crime. It would be surprising to learn that while we are in the throes of a probe to Mars the law lacks the will and know-how to reach the upper floors of a corporate skyscraper.

The Harm

The damage done by victimless crimes to the 'moral fabric' of society is taken as a given, without rational explanation or historical evidence. Over the centuries, the criminal justice system has expended most of its energy, time and resources prosecuting them. Enlightened communities that have progressively consigned harmless criminality to the dustbin of legal history still await that moral decay promised by legal moralism. It must be comforting to the denizens of Los Angeles to know that they have been spared moral decline through the vigilance and zeal of their vice squads, whereas the inhabitants of Sydney must await the predicted fall of the sunny skies over New South Wales upon those long, warm, barbecued summer days.

This preoccupation with the sins of the flesh is rooted in our past. Both church and state found carnality fertile ground for exploitation. Such sins were singled out and stigmatised long ago while, in the words of Ross:

> The prosperous evildoers that bask undisturbed in popular favour have been careful to shun – or seem to shun – the familiar types of wickedness. Overlooked in Bible and prayer book, their obliquities lack the brimstone smell. Surpass as their misdeeds may in meanness and cruelty, there has not yet been time enough to store up strong emotion about them; and so the sight of them does not let loose the flood of wrath and abhorrence that rushes down upon the long-attainted sins.[9]

Showing no similar interest in fraudulent behaviour (before the latter half of the eighteenth century, the common law considered it absurd that a person should be indicted for making a fool of another), the criminal law has surrendered its original jurisdiction over white-collar offenders to governmental and quasi-governmental agencies, leaving the police to deal with, in the words of Ross again, 'their low-browed cousins' who 'occupy … the steerage of society.'[10]

Incongruously, Western culture has always prided itself on its values of honesty, integrity and the incorruptibility of its institutions, virtues underpinning that trust so indispensable to any functional society, and which is the first casualty of white-collar crime. As Sutherland observes:

> White-collar crimes violate trust and therefore create distrust, which lowers social morale and produces social disorganisation on a large scale. Other crimes produce relatively little effect on social institutions or social organization.[11]

The truth of this observation is apparent and easily measured in a small and relatively confined environment such as academia, where any suspicion regarding the integrity of the examination process (be it cheating, disclosure of questions or biased marking) is utterly destructive of student morale. Yet, in an astonishing programme put out by Australian television in 2003, a number of sports stars were paraded reminiscing, with amusement, upon the occasions when they had cheated in exams. The damage done by

---

[9] *Sin and Society*, p.47.
[10] Ibid.
[11] *White-Collar Crime*, revised edition, 1977, p.42.

such a broadcast is exacerbated, if this is possible, by the known fact that sporting personalities are significant role models for the young. Justified or not, in the opinion of Walter Lippman, those in public life 'are the custodians of a nation's ideals, of the beliefs it cherishes, of its permanent hopes.'[12]

Before WorldCom and Enron it was thought that we would never again witness the excesses that in 1961 engulfed Westinghouse and General Electric (both household names), involving secret meetings, destruction of evidence, codes and fictitious names, rivalling the very best television coverage of organised crime – but lacking, of course, that frisson created by armed police and manacled felons. Of the forty-five conspirators implicated, only seven served a prison term – a trifling thirty days apiece – and in light of progress so far in the current spate of corporate collapse, these can be considered unlucky.[13] This is remarkable if one compares the growing concern in recent years for the health of the natural environment. There is no lack of political will in tackling perceived threats to endangered species, the ozone layer and clean air, but these corporate behemoths, imperilling the human environment, remain unrestrained much as were their predecessors in the vertebrate world of Jurassic times.

The spectacle of the powerful and influential 'getting away with it' is not only demoralising but essentially criminogenic. A sense of injustice, that there is one law for the rich and another for the poor, is dangerously alienating, inculcating feelings of frustration and helplessness, and leading to much serious antisocial behaviour and reactive criminality. The unpalatable truth is that organised crime has flourished not only because of the law's intransigence regarding harmless criminality, an area of personal need and high demand, but also because of its more general failure to be even-handed. Al Capone's remark about 'the legitimate rackets' is no mere wisecrack. It speaks volumes about the impunity of power in our society, as does the humorous comment regarding the best way to rob a bank. Robbery is not a very cost-effective method, whereas corporate corruption, used as

---

[12] Ibid. p.211 (from the *New York Times*, 15 December 1974, p.17).
[13] The impact of the American Sarbanes-Oxley legislation is discussed pp.68–69.

a weapon, is demonstrably more effective than the knife or gun.

The tendency for frustration to explode in unacceptable violence is all too often apparent in racially motivated riots. It was also evident in a particularly unpleasant sexual assault committed on a white woman with the muzzle of a firearm in apartheid-era South Africa some years ago. It was revealed during the trial that the offender, a coloured man (of mixed race), who was hanged for the offence, had for no obvious reason been picked up and assaulted by the police earlier in the day.

The problem with the confrontational approach is that human existence is regarded as a battleground of winners and losers, of success or failure. This is a superficial perception which distorts the reality of human relationships and appears to draw its inspiration from a misapprehension of the natural world. Depicting a condition of predator and prey, it overlooks those cooperative strategies within species, involving selflessness and give and take, which play such a significant role in ensuring survival.

When Kipling's twin impostors fill the view, the unscrupulous procure advantage by purchasing political favour, suborning associates and engendering ethical subcultures at odds with those of the community at large. All institutions, organisations and political and professional bodies are at risk of evolving deviant codes of practice similar to those of the so-called 'criminal underworld'. From time to time, these have endured scandals revealing extraordinary behaviour by conditioned members working in an environment where independent ethical judgment is discouraged. In the corporate world, what is required is 'a good organisation man', one prepared to condone conduct involving deception and misrepresentation unthinkable in the real world of community, friends and family. This 'ethical numbing', discussed by Coleman,[14] involves not only a personal conflict between work and home, but constitutes a growing threat to that great engine of liberty and progress from cave to cafeteria, capitalism itself. Recent corporate corruption revealing venal carnivores in industry, commercial banks, auditors and consultants, both legal and financial, feeding off the system which has bestowed so much

---

[14] *White-Collar Crime Reconsidered*, Chapter 2.

favour upon them, has led to a damaging loss of trust and headlong flight to the relative safety of bricks and mortar.

The past decade has witnessed a typical example of the impact of economic downturn on law enforcement. On the one hand, there was a loosening of control by the agencies charged with upholding ethical standards, in an attempt to nurture economic growth by stimulating business activity, and on the other, a tightening of punitive action, through zero tolerance campaigns, against traditional crime because of perceived threats to social stability resulting from unemployment and increasingly disadvantaged groups. In the former Soviet Union, crimes of the market-place were regarded as particularly heinous, and treated more severely than traditional crime, as they constituted a direct threat to the socio-economic system. However, with the end of the cold war, the region experienced a chaotic period of unbridled commercial and political corruption, so massive as to cause a sudden decline in the life expectancy of the average Russian. Disappointingly, the reaction was the familiar law and order crackdown at street level, involving, predictably, the wholesale round-up of prostitutes.

In a 1997 report appearing in *The Sunday Times*,[15] an enthusiastic police captain commissioned by Moscow's mayor (aspiring to fill Boris Yeltsin's shoes) ahead of an international mayoral conference, exclaimed, 'It was a great catch. We came back with a whole busload. We are arresting several hundred girls every night … This is the new Moscow. The authorities want it to be clean and upright – the best city in the world.'

This utterly superficial response to widespread social and economic distress has for too long conferred the trappings of respectability. Reminiscent of the function of street cleansing departments and much of the thinking underlying campaigns of 'zero tolerance', such a response brings reassurance to the Pharisee who ignores the biblical teaching that Jesus forgave the prostitute, defended the woman found in adultery and promised the good Samaritan eternal life, but cast out the money-changers from the temple.

Understandably, offences involving violence are the most

---

[15] 15 June 1997 (UK).

feared, particularly by the more physically vulnerable female, and incur the most severe penalties. However, it would be erroneous to assume that white-collar crime confines itself to inflicting economic harm, severe though the ramifications of serious financial loss to both mental and physical well-being may prove to be. Quite the opposite is true. Echoing the sentiments of Aristotle, Braithwaite has pointed out:

> Work since Sutherland leaves little doubt that more of the most serious crimes that cause the greatest property loss and the greatest physical injury are perpetrated by the rich than by the poor.[16]

This is because wealth gives access to power which delivers the means of causing human misery on a larger scale. In any given year, white-collar crime causes proprietary loss many times greater than run-of-the-mill traditional offences such as housebreaking and theft. For example, it is estimated that the fraud involved in the collapse of Enron runs into billions of dollars, more than the GNP of some nation states. But the same can also be said of the body count in death and injury occasioned by white-collar criminality compared with that of all traditional violent crime. Entire communities have been exposed to carcinogenic substances that have 'escaped' into the environment, or been poisoned by industrial effluent or sewage, as happened in Walkerton, Ontario through a failure (followed by concealment) to safeguard the domestic water supply.

The workplace is particularly dangerous. So-called 'industrial accidents', which are frequently not the result of mischance at all, daily exact their deadly toll. Most of these are not of a scale sufficient to attract headlines such as Bhopal and the Challenger[17] and Columbia disasters, but many share the same origin, namely an alleged failure to observe safety requirements in order to maximise short-term profits. It is, of course, impossible to provide for every exigency – one of the most worrying being the concealment by operatives of a drink or drugs problem – and

---

[16] *White-Collar Crime Reconsidered,* Chapter 3, p.78.
[17] Ibid. Discussed by Kramer, p.214.

curbs on costs, including maintenance (the calls upon which, like health, are bottomless) are essential if an enterprise is to remain viable; but this does not excuse calculated disregard for established minimum safety standards.

In America, it is alleged, more people die from unnecessary surgical procedures than from firearms.[18] In England, at the same time that Divine Brown, having been kept under surveillance subsequent to her release, was pursued and rearrested in another state on a further prostitution charge,[19] a dentist who had maimed a number of female patients by carrying out unwarranted, though highly lucrative, dental work was merely recalled for 'retraining' (sic. restraining). No prosecution for assault, although permanent damage and disfigurement had been caused, was ever contemplated, and the professional body concerned, which would have unceremoniously struck off any member who touched a female patient inappropriately, admitted after inquiry that they had no idea of his present whereabouts.

Thousands of haemophiliacs have died from AIDS or await a lingering death, having been transfused with blood known to constitute a risk in order to avoid the financial loss of discarding existing untreated stocks. In Japan, senior Green Cross executives were at least prosecuted for such behaviour,[20] albeit only for professional negligence carrying paltry terms of imprisonment; but elsewhere such persons have escaped liability altogether, in one case being rewarded with senior positions in prestigious English institutions.

This inability to rein in dangerous predators at arm's length in time and place is due in large part to the culture shock to a society conditioned to associating violent crime with a physical one-on-one, even face-to-face, confrontation involving bloodstained putty knife or brides in a bath, leaving it unable to accommodate remoter, dispassionate, impersonal villainy. The choice of emotive and misleading language, for example 'malice' or 'manslaughter', is equally unhelpful. Even the rules themselves, such as the narrowing of the meaning of intention to exclude

---

[18] See *The Rich get Richer and the Poor get Prison*, pp.61–3.
[19] *The Daily Telegraph* (UK), 12 December 1996.
[20] *Sydney Morning Herald*, 25 February 2000.

those who knowingly place others at risk, and the now absurd provision (traceable to the Statute of Gloucester, 1278), required in all homicides, that death ensue within a year and a day (thereby ruling out all cases of prolonged demise), inhibit the necessary adjustment.

Such language and limitation are predicated on some form of physical attack, and it should be noted that the 'abolition' of the year and a day rule[21] (quite properly not retrospective in its operation) merely extends the period to three years, beyond which prosecution is subject not to law but discretionary power. In the years ahead it will be interesting to see how the discretion of the Attorney-General is exercised where the victim succumbs to, say, asbestosis or AIDS long after exposure. However, even if the system were no longer prepared to pass off this tally of death and injury as a matter for fines and private litigation, and acquired the political will to prosecute at public expense as a first, not a last, resort with indictment for assault and homicide, followed by incarceration, there is no more room. The prisons are filled to overflowing with conventional offenders confined by the political imperative of 'getting tough on crime'.

On any given day in the land of the free, just over 2 million Americans are behind bars, with a further 4½ million on parole or probation. This is the highest prison population in the world (at 701 per 100,000), almost five times that of Australia (at 153 per 100,000) where there is growing concern at an increase which compares unfavourably with the UK (at 141 per 100,000).[22] On their release, with inadequate or no in-house programmes of rehabilitation and assistance outside limited to a suit of clothes, ten dollars and a one-way bus ticket, 75% are rearrested within three years. The result is that, of the entire population of the United States, one in twenty white, and one in five black males have been in prison, a situation reminiscent of the convict settlements in early Australia. But the similarity ends there. Most inmates come out as they went in, functionally illiterate, mentally disordered or with a serious drug

---

[21] Law Reform (Year and a Day Rule) Act 1996.
[22] Admittedly, the inclusion of work outreach camps and community custody centres in Queensland within the scope of the Prisoner Census in 2003 has partly contributed to this increase.

problem – but with the additional handicap of a criminal record which, if for felony, bars them in some states from various types of employment and the right to vote. And in many instances they are infected with AIDS or TB.[23]

Since it is agreed that the main purpose of punishment is deterrence and that, leaving aside the contentious issue of the death penalty, the threat of imprisonment is the most feared sanction of all, it might have been thought that white-collar criminals were prime candidates for the threat of incarceration,[24] being peculiarly susceptible to social disgrace, accustomed to comfortable living conditions and considering the premeditation of their offences. Nevertheless, it is not deemed appropriate to condemn the better class of person to such a fate. Confronted by the most serious internal threat in our history, Nero-like, the forces of law and order continue to pursue the hobgoblin of carnal sin – in America, by locking up drug users, prostitutes and women convicted of 'raping' their teenage lovers; in England, by debating the number and nature of warnings to be issued by police to soliciting males and whether or not places of resort located near universities and military bases should be characterised as 'brothels' despite the fact that the ladies in attendance charge no fee for their services. A reading of these judgments questioning the need for any commercial element (exposing, for example, any hotelier or landlord who fails to demand production of a marriage licence to prosecution) serves as a chilling reminder of the medieval moralism of the English judiciary.

As long ago as 1939, Sutherland raised the alarm in his presidential address to the American Sociological Society:

> The crimes of the lower class are handled by policemen, prosecutors and judges with penal sanctions in the form of fines, imprisonment, and death. The crimes of the upper class either result in no official action at all, or result in suits for damages in civil courts, or are handled by inspectors and by administrative boards or commissions with penal sanctions in the form of

---

[23] Source: *The Economist*, 10–16 August 2002, p.13 and pp.27–8; Home Office Research, Development and Statistics Directorate 2003, London; Australian Bureau of Statistics, 'Prisoners in Australia', June 2003.

[24] This was the view of the Committee on Economic Offences of the American Bar Association's Section on Criminal Justice, reporting in 1977, p.8.

warnings, orders to cease and desist, occasionally the loss of a licence, and only in extreme cases by fines or prison sentences.[25]

One of the 'extreme cases' envisaged by Sutherland would presumably be the Watergate scandal of 1972–1975. The corporate executives implicated in this *cause célèbre* continued to preside over their companies (though admittedly, all were fined small amounts of less than two thousand dollars, and two did 'time' of less than three months), whereas, it should be recalled, that Heidi Fleiss was sentenced to three years in gaol on the pandering charge alone, and Divine Brown, bearing in mind her comparatively meagre earnings, paid a much heavier fine and served a term of six months' imprisonment. Obviously, a conspiracy to undermine the independence of the electoral process and thereby threaten the basis of democratic government was considered of less moment than the provision of sexual services – plainly regarded as 'a clear and present danger'. Oliver Wendell Holmes, an eminent American jurist, once remarked that the types of behaviour which a society seeks to prevent reveals the values of that society.[26]

It remains to be seen whether the Sarbanes-Oxley legislation, enacted during the panicky aftermath of the most recent spate of corporate scandals in America, represents a dramatic turnaround in entrenched values or a passing ritual sacrifice of a chosen few to appease the wrath of the marketplace (with its hungry investors and grossly inflated expectations). Those condemned to the arena have received prison sentences measured in years instead of the days and weeks previously imposed for the same malpractice, and comparable to those convicted of terrorist activity, on the evidence of erstwhile colleagues hoping to limit their own exposure. It must be said that the signs of a change of heart are not encouraging. The offending corporations themselves have been spared, thereby saving jobs and investment, as have the collaborating merchant banks and lawyers – on the ground that they merely aided and abetted the frauds involved! – and the

---

[25] *White-Collar Crime*, revised edition, 1977, p.45.
[26] 'Law in Science and Science in Law', *Collected Legal Papers*, Harcourt Bruce, 1921, p.212.

deeply mired auditors seem destined to be let off the hook because of the worsening concentration of the audit industry, already reduced to the 'Big Four' with the demise of Arthur Andersen. This singling out of a few for exemplary punishment is a cause for dismay. It not only projects a distorted image of a false messiah leading astray his blameless disciples, but also represents the repudiation of an opportunity to expose the root cause of the problem, namely, the malpractice engendered by deviant subcultures.

All this smacks of expediency and the adoption of a cost-benefit approach to the white-collar community, in marked contrast to that directed at conventional crime, particularly the reckless pursuit of harmless criminality rendering the cure worse than the ailment, redolent with moralism and the notion of just desserts. It is already being questioned, as a result of such cost-benefit analysis, whether the aim of restoring confidence in corporate America might have been better served by adopting the hitherto preferred option of civil rather than criminal proceedings.

Epilogue

All students of constitutional law learn of the doctrine of the 'separation of powers', but we neglect an earlier and wiser teaching: 'Render unto Caesar the things that are Caesar's and unto God the things that are God's.'[1]

Adopting the sentiments of Mill, Hart and the Wolfenden Committee, an attempt has been made to demonstrate that, apart from any question of disobedience, it is distasteful, inappropriate and counter-productive for the criminal law to embroil itself in moralistic and religious issues. Its proper function is to devote its undivided attention to those in our midst who are dangerous; those who would harm us in our person or property. Arguably, the two most potent motivating forces in human nature are the sex drive and the pursuit of wealth, yet they have received wholly disparate treatment at the hands of the criminal justice system. The former, in all its manifestations, has been persecuted for centuries while the latter, however damaging its impact, has been ignored or treated with deference. This disposal mocks a society which over many thousands of years, and against the odds, has achieved a culture in which the values of honesty, integrity and trust are regarded as indispensable; so much so that we find it impossible to envisage a state of affairs where lying, cheating and betrayal were acceptable features of daily life.

Drastic changes are called for if the criminal law is to stop sending out the wrong message. Harmless crimes, now fashionably termed 'quality of life' offences (though whose quality of life is being considered is difficult to determine) must be recognised for what they are – a recrudescence from a wayward religious past. Police forces must be rid of corruption (though much temptation will be removed by the legalisation of the remaining harmless activities), and the bobby on the beat must be

---

[1] Jesus responding to a question put by a group of Pharisees. Mark 12:17.

supplemented by officers trained to be a match for white-collar criminality. The adversarial system, already the odd man out, must be abandoned and replaced by some variant of the inquisitorial model. The judicial control of sentencing should be handed over to a panel of lay persons representative of interested groups, recruited from the community at large. After all, those historically drawn from the ranks of counsel who have carved out their careers tasked, not infrequently, with defending the indefensible, are hardly best qualified to rule on what amounts to just desserts. The significance of the nature and quantum of the punishment handed down cannot be overestimated, as it must not only assuage the wrath of those aggrieved and bring closure to the bereaved, but also indirectly reward the law-abiding for their self-denial.

Earlier this year a man from Blacktown in New South Wales,[2] knowing he was infected with the AIDS virus, nevertheless passed on the deadly disease to two women through unprotected sexual intercourse obtained by lying to them about his condition. When he was brought before the Penrith Court charged with maliciously causing a grievous bodily disease (an offence specifically designed by an amended Crimes Act to deal with just such a situation) the charge was dropped on the grounds that it was considered impossible to prove that the accused intended to communicate the disease. How could such a grotesque result come about?

St Augustine once said of 'time' that it was a notion understood by everyone until asked. Much the same can be said about 'intention'. What do we mean by saying that a harmful consequence was intended? Remarkably, although this state of mind – whatever it is – is required for all serious crimes such as murder, sexual assault and fraud, yet over centuries, the English common law has not come up with an answer. Is it foresight of harm, or one's motive or desire, or is it simply purpose? Due to the overriding need to distinguish murder (which requires intention) from the lesser form of homicide, termed manslaughter (which requires, in one of its many forms, recklessness – the essence of which is foresight), all reference to the presence or absence of

---

[2] Reported in the *Sydney Morning Herald*, 14 February 2005.

such foresight has been expunged from the meaning of intention. Again, motive and desire, the reason for or cause of action, has always been irrelevant to the verdict of guilt or innocence, but may well be significant at the later stage when the appropriate sentence is considered. For example, a loving mother may kill her disabled child to spare it further suffering, or a corporate executive may defraud investors in order to benefit his company.

This leaves us with purpose which, according to Lord Bridge in the leading case of Moloney,[3] is too narrow, as it excludes the man who, in order to evade imminent arrest, boards a plane bound for Manchester. Although it is not his purpose to travel to that destination, Lord Bridge is at pains to stress that, nevertheless, he intends to do so. On the analogy of this example, it appears that the Blacktown man, whose objective was none other than unprotected sex, nevertheless intended to infect the women. Indeed, communication of the disease was far more certain than arrival in Manchester, which could have been aborted by eventualities such as a sudden adverse change in weather conditions (not unknown in that part of the world) or engine failure. Queen Victoria is said to have once exclaimed, when squeezed between competing interests, 'My Lords you seat me but narrowly!' But the Law Lords have managed to leave no room for intention at all. How much simpler it would be, and more in accord with common expectation, to follow the Roman-Dutch-based South African Law[4] and apply the broad sweep of *dolus eventualis* – the German concept which finds intention whenever an actor foresees an outcome and reconciles himself to its occurrence.

Although taken for granted, our highest achievement, not to be surpassed, is the creation of a finely tuned conscience: that awareness of right and wrong; that appreciation of what is fair and what is unjust. Now at the end of the journey, we are equipped to pass judgment on whether or not the Anglo-American criminal justice system nurtures this priceless attribute.

---

[3] [1985] AC 905.
[4] See Jensen J A in *S v Ngubane* 1985 (3) SA 677(A)

Bibliography

Aristotle, *Politics* trans. Welldon, JEC, Macmillan, 1932.

Drucker, Ernest, 'Just Say No to America' in *Sydney Morning Herald*, 6 March 2006.

Economist, 10 August 2002, pp.10–16.

Erickson, KT, *Wayward Puritans*, John Wiley and Sons, 1966.

FBI Uniform Crime Report, 1973 and 2001.

Geis, Gilbert and Meier, Robert F, *White-Collar Crime: Offences in Business, Politics and the Professions*, The Free Press, 1977.

Glanville Williams, *The Proof of Guilt*, Stevens and Sons, 1963.

Hart, H L A, *Law Liberty and Morality*, Oxford University Press, 1962.

Hart, H L A, *The Morality of the Criminal Law*, Oxford University Press, 1965.

HMSO, *Report of the Committee on Homosexual Offences and Prostitution*, Cmnd 247, 1957.

Holmes, Oliver Wendell, 'Law in Science and Science in Law' in *Collected Legal Papers*, Harcourt Bruce, 1921.

Home Office, 'Paying the Price', consultation document, July 2004.

Hoskins, George L, *Law and Authority in Early Massachusetts*, Macmillan, 1960.

Journal of Criminal Law and Criminology, Symposium: 'Why Is Crime Decreasing?' vol. 88 no. 4, Northwestern University School of Law, 1988.

Kinsey, Alfred, Pomeroy, Wardell B and Martin, Clyde E, *Sexual Behaviour in the Human Male*, Saunders, 1948.

Meier, Robert F and Geis, Gilbert, *Victimless Crime?* Roxbury Publishing Company, 1997.

Mencken, H L, *In Defense of Women*, Alfred A Knopf, 1922.

Mill, John Stuart, *On Liberty*, London, 1859.

Morris, Norval, 'Crimes Without Victims: The Law is a Busybody' in *New York Times*, 18 January 1973.

Morris, Norval and Hawkins, Gordon, *The Honest Politician's Guide to Crime Control*, University of Chicago Press, 1970.

Packer, Herbert L, *The Limits of the Criminal Sanction*, Stanford University Press, 1968.

Reiman, T H, *The Rich Get Richer and the Poor Get Prison,* John Wiley and Sons, 1984.

Rook, P and Ward, R, *Rook and Ward on Sexual Offences*, Sweet and Maxwell, 1977.

Ross, Edward A, *Sin and Society*, Houghton Mifflin, 1907.

Schlegal, Kip and Weisburd, David, *White-Collar Crime Reconsidered*, Northeastern University Press, 1992.

Schur, Edwin M and Bedau, H, *Victimless Crimes*, Prentice Hall, 1974.

Stenton, F M, 'Anglo-Saxon England' in *Oxford History of England Vol II*, Clarendon Press, 1971.

Waugh, Auberon, *The Sunday Telegraph* (UK), 25 October 1988.

www.ingramcontent.com/pod-product-compliance
Lightning Source LLC
Chambersburg PA
CBHW031541210526
45464CB00003B/1088